SOME ASPESTS OF EDUCATION IN ANCIENT INDIA

Owing to the antiquity and rarity of this book, certain pages are regrettably absent, and readability is compromised due to the blurring of the original text. If you possess any insights regarding the availability of these missing sections, kindly inform us. Your assistance is crucial in ensuring the completion of this significant work for the benefit of future generations.

SOME ASPESTS OF EDUCATION IN ANCIENT INDIA

C. KUNHAN RAJA

GYAN

Published by

Gyan Publishing House
5, Ansari Road
Daryaganj, New Delhi-110002
Phone: 011-47034999, 9811692060
E-mail: books@gyanbooks.com

Distribution Network
gyanbooks.com
India, USA, Canada, UK, Australia

ISBN: 978-93-7316-056-6 (PB)

First Published, 1950

2nd Impression 2025

Printed at: Gyan Press, Delhi.

SOME ASPESTS OF EDUCATION IN ANCIENT INDIA
Author: C. KUNHAN RAJA

The Adyar Library Series—No. 73

GENERAL EDITOR:

DR. G. SRINIVASA MURTI, B.A., B.L., M.B. & C.M., VAIDYARATNA

Director, Adyar Library

SOME ASPECTS OF EDUCATION IN ANCIENT INDIA

SOME ASPECTS OF EDUCATION IN ANCIENT INDIA

(DEWAN BAHADUR K. KRISHNASWAMI RAO ENDOWMENT LECTURES IN THE UNIVERSITY OF MADRAS, 17TH AND 18TH NOVEMBER, 1949)

BY

DR. C. KUNHAN RAJA

Professor of Sanskrit, University of Madras

THE ADYAR LIBRARY

1950

PREFACE

I MUST first of all thank the Vice-Chancellor and the Syndicate of the University of Madras for giving me an opportunity to deliver this course of lectures under an endowment bearing the name of a person who has taken great interest in ancient Indian culture. I still recollect the time when he was the Dewan of Travancore. I know also institutions which owe their origin and development to the love and enthusiasm which he had for ancient Indian culture.

I have already published about half a dozen articles on the subject of ancient Indian education, in some journals and in some Commemoration Volumes. I also delivered the Convocation Address of the Sanskrit College in Jaipur early in 1947, in Sanskrit, on the same subject. All of them are published.

In this course I have tried to develop certain aspects which are only touched upon in some of the previous contributions of mine relating to this subject, and in dealing with the subject I cannot avoid some occasional repetition of a few of the points already dealt with elsewhere.

I have tried to show the correct meaning of the terms *Brahmacārin* and *Upanayana*, in different contexts, and I have also shown the difference between *Upanayana* and *Upasadana*, which both precede the student's study under a teacher.

I have dealt with four stages in the education of a boy, and I have dealt with the advanced academic activities of scholars. The four stages are the elementary education at home, the education in the household of the teacher in a lower and in a higher stage, and the highly specialised education. I have also tried to clear the question of the duration of the various courses of study.

I have made an effort to show the unity and continuity of tradition relating to education from the early *Vedic* times to even recent times, through the periods of the *Brāhmaṇas*, the *Āraṇyakas*, the *Upaniṣads*, the *Sūtras* the *Smṛtis*, etc. I have also explained the obligatory and universal nature of the education of a high standard, in the country.

This obligatory education was meant to equip the boys to be worthy citizens of the State. The prominence given to *Yāgas* and to *Brahman*-knowledge as the sole objective kept in this obligatory education is a later phase. It was only one of the objects in the study at the teacher's household.

Towards the end I have dealt with certain minor points like the life of the students, the forest institutions and women's education. Practically the lectures form a cursory commentary on the prescription, "One shall study what has been prescribed for one's own study" in the *Taittirīyāraṇyaka*. I have considered this prescription in the light of the *Gṛhya-Sūtras* besides citing passages from the *Brāhmaṇas* the *Āraṇyakas* and the *Upaniṣads*. I have also discussed the scope of the opening *Sūtras* in the *Mīmāṁsā* and the *Vedānta* systems in the light of the general tendency of the instruction given by the teacher to the student at the end of his study course, found in the *Taittirīyopaniṣad*. I have made use of relevent remarks in the *Bhāṣya* of S'abarasvāmin, the *Vārtika* of Kumārila Bhaṭṭa and the *S'āstra-Dīpikā* of Pārthasārathi Misra, in the *Mīmāṁsā S'āstra*.

I have given the translations of the cited passages in the body of the book, and I have given the text as foot-notes. The translations are my own. In some cases I have given both the Sanskrit word and the corresponding English word in the body of the book itself. When a word has been used a large number of times, I have not given the terms in both the languages on later occasions. I take it that the readers would have become familiar with the terms through constant use.

Sri K. Balasubrahmanya Ayyar and Dewan Bahadur K. S. Ramaswami Sastrigal took the chair on the two days of the lectures and I am very grateful to them for this honour. I also thank all the people who were kind enough to attend the lectures. The Adyar Library has kindly agreed to publish the lectures in their Series, and the University has given the necessary permission. The Vasanta Press has printed the book very expeditiously and at the same time without any fall from their usual standard in printing and get up. I thank all the people concerned for their help.

University of Madras C. KUNHAN RAJA
1st March, 1950

POSTSCRIPT

WHEN this book was going through the Press, I was suddenly called away to Iran to take up the post of Professor of Sanskrit in the Institute of Languages of the Iran University(*Anjuman-e-Iran Shinashi*), Teheran. I had to leave India before the printing was finished. My colleagues in the Adyar Library helped me in getting the book through the Press and finishing the printing, during my absence. I thank them for this help.

C. K. R.

CONTENTS

SOME ASPECTS OF EDUCATION IN ANCIENT INDIA

LECTURE I

I. Preliminary

In this course of lectures, just two in number, I do not propose to enter into a detailed discussion of the various points relating to education in ancient India. It is an impossibility, having regard to the narrow compass available. Further, a few books have already been written by other scholars, which deal with the various points in a detailed way; and it is not necessary to duplicate the work. It is not even possible here to bring in all the points relating to the subject, although there is no book now available where all the facts have been assembled together and arranged in an orderly way. What has been done in the earlier works is only to discuss the points and to give the relevant facts in foot-notes. I have already collected a large number of such points myself, and perhaps at a later stage I may attempt to arrange them in some definite order and to present them in the form of a separate book.

My object in this course of lectures is to discuss a few important points. When it comes to the matter of interpretation, my own feeling is that the facts have not been correctly presented in any book till now published. There has always been a demand to make education in India truly Indian both in form and in spirit, and in the few extracts I have seen from the views expressed by the chairman of the University Commission recently appointed by the Government of India, the ideal which the framers of the Report have before them is to present a scheme whereby Indians could be educated in an Indian way[1]. If such an ideal is to be worked out, we must know what the true Indian ideals are in education. We must also know whether there is any fundamental difference between such ideals and the ideals of what I will call "the universal system of education", *i.e.*, a system of education fitted for ***man*** and not for the citizens of any particular State.

There are various ways in which the problem could be handled. We can take up the subject according to the various aspects of education and consider

[1] The passage is: To judge from the observations made by the Chairman of the Commission at the Press Conference, the general approach of the Commission to the entire problem of education has been sound. He said that one of the main objectives which the Commission kept in view was "to make our education more Indian in character than it has been." In all free countries, education is imparted with a background of the history and culture of the respective countries. "But in this country for a long time, our education has been more or less on un-Indian lines." Our education must shed the un-Indian influences.

each one of the aspects in a historical way. We can also take up the whole subject in a historical way and consider each of the aspects in the various stages in this historical evolution of educational system in the country. Whatever be the approach, it is not possible to keep up the plan absolutely. We will have to stray away from the path occasionally. What I propose to do is to have a combination of both the modes of approach. On the whole I propose to take up the entire subject in a historical way; but it will be necessary for me to proceed with a point to a later stage before finishing the other aspects.

II. Saṁhitās

The *Rigveda* represents the earliest stage in the history of India for which we have any literary record. When we take up the *Rigvedic* period, I must confess that the material available is very scanty. One will look into the *Rigveda* in vain for terms like *Ācārya* and *Guru* (Teacher), *S'iṣya* and *Antevāsin* (disciples), *Ās'ramas* (Hermitages) and so on, that are intimately connected with education. There is the word *Guru* in the *Rigveda*; but it does not mean Teacher at all, in it. We know much about the religion and philosophy of the *Rigvedic* times, from the text itself. There are frequent references to family relationships like father and son, brother and sister, husband and wife and so on. The relation between the king and the people is also frequently mentioned. Cities and villages, clans and communities, wealth, poetry, music and other arts, sports and pastimes and various other subjects are also mentioned in the text. But we get practically nothing about the relation of Teacher and student in the *Rigveda*.

From the absence of any reference to writing in the *Vedas*, Max Muller concluded that writing came to be known in India only at a much later period.[1] Macdonell, with a sense of humour, has said that we should not stretch the arguments based on silence too far, in as much as there is no mention of salt in the *Rigveda*; from that are we to conclude that the *Rigvedic* people had only a saltless diet?[2] There is no doubt about the intellectual eminence of the *Rigvedic* Aryans. And such eminence is not confined to a few select prodigies as an accident. The general level must also have been very high; it is impossible that such prodigies should flourish in an intellectual desert. And is it possible that there should he such a high level of intellectualism in the average person unless there was also a high system of education?

Although there is no direct mention of education in the *Rigveda*, there are certain ways in which we can know something about the mode of education at that time from indirect sources. We are all familiar with

[1] History of Ancient Sanskrit Literature, pp. 497 ff.

[2] This is what he said when he was dealing with the point in the class. K. F. Geldner too held the view that writing must have been known to the *Vedic* Aryas, having regard to the high level of the culture.

the famous sentence in the *Taittirīyāraṇyaka*, " One should study what has been prescribed for his own study."[1] This comes at a very late stage in the *Vedic* period, in the middle of the *Taittirīyāraṇyaka (Prapāṭhaka* II, *Anuvāka* 15). There is one passage in the *Rigveda* which proves that, although the definite mention of education is only in such a late work as the *Taittirīyāraṇyaka*, the idea contained in it is a far earlier one, that the *Svādhyāyādhyayana* (study of what has been prescribed for one's own study), as understood by the passage was the custom even in the *Rigvedic* times. The passage is :

> When among them one (frog) repeats the words of the other like a student that of the teacher.[2]
>
> (Rigveda VII-103-5)

This is a hymn describing the frogs in the rainy season. In this passage there is a clear reference to one frog repeating the words of another frog like students studying the *Vedas* from a teacher. What is contained in the prescription of study in the *Taittirīyāraṇyaka* is this kind of study of the recitation of the *Veda* by a student from the teacher. There have been some attempts in recent times to discover a sort of social, religious and philosophical " evolution " from the *Rigveda* onwards, along with a language evolution also. But from a comparison of the direct statement

[1] स्वाध्यायोऽध्येतव्यः ।

[2] यदेषामन्यो अन्यस्य वाचं शाक्तस्येव वदति शिक्षमाणः ॥

about study contained in the prescription of study in the *Taittirīyāraṇyaka* and the indirect reference to such a system of study by rote in the *Rigveda*, we know that there has been no material change from the *Rigvedic* times to the time of the *Taittirīyāraṇyaka*, in point of the system of education. In this way, although it is not possible to get any direct statement about education in the *Rigveda*, we know that all that is meant by the prescription of "one's own study" in the *Taittirīyāraṇyaka* must have been current in the *Rigvedic* times, from this one solitary reference in an indirect way.

We should realise that we have in the *Rigveda* only a very small part of the literature that must have existed at that time, and what actually existed at that time must have been an immense wealth. The extent *Rigveda* is only about half the size of the *Rāmāyaṇa*. Therefore even this solitary reference means a lot to us. It is true that there are words in the *Rigveda* which mean " teaching ". Thus there are places where the forms of the root *S'ās* mean " to teach ", " to inform ". There are also words which actually mean " Teacher " :

> Iḷā they made the Teacher of the sons of men.[1]
>
> (Rigveda I-31-11).

Here the word translated as " Teacher " is ***s'āsanīm***, from the root *S'ās*. There are also places where the word ***s'āsana*** means only " control " as in :

[1] इळामकृण्वन् मनुषस्य शासनीम् ।

They know the red Bull's blessings and are joyful under the flaming coloured Lord's control.[1]

(Rigveda III-7-5)

The root *S'ās* has continued its meaning of "instruction" in words like *Anus'āsana* and *S'āstra*. This is a *Rigvedic* sense of the root. Thus some kind of teaching or instruction must have been a prominent element in the *Rigvedic* life; to this extent we can be on sure ground. What I meant was that an actual reference to any details relating to the mode of teaching and to the relation of teacher and disciple is missing in the *Rigveda*; there is only the indirect allusion in the hymn on frogs, from which I have already given the passage. There are other passages also in the hymn where there is reference to the recitation of the *Vedic Mantras* in the *Yagas*.[2] From these we also know that

[1] जानन्ति वृष्णो अरुषस्य शेवमुत ब्रध्नस्य शासने रणन्ति ॥

[2] संवत्सरं शशयाना ब्राह्मणा व्रतचारिणः ।
वाचं पर्जन्यजिन्वितं प्र मण्डूका अवादिषुः ॥ (VII. 103.1)

The Brahmins who observe their vows, who lay quiet for a year, the frogs have spoken out their voice, inspired by Parjanya.

ब्राह्मणासो अतिरात्रे न सोमे सरो न पूर्णं अभितो वदन्तः ।
संवत्सरस्य तदहः परिष्ठ यन्मण्डूकाः प्रावृषीणं बभूव ॥ (VII. 103.7)

As Brahmins sitting round the brimful lake (*soma* vessel) sing at the *Soma* rite of *Atirātra*, so the frogs, ye gather round (the lake) this day the first of the rainy season.

ब्राह्मणासः सोमिनो वाचमक्रत ब्रह्म कृण्वन्तः परिवत्सरीणम् ।
अध्वर्यवो घर्मिणः सिष्विदाना आविर्भवन्ति गुह्या न केचित् ॥ (VII. 103.8)

These Brahmins with the *soma* juice performing their year-long rite, have sung out; and these performers of rite (*Adhvaryus*) sweating with their kettles, show themselves; and none are hidden.

the learning of the *Vedic Mantras* has the performance of the *Yāgas* (sacrifices) as the purpose.

Associated with the prescription of one's own study are *Upanayana* and *Brahmacarya* (usually translated as "studentship"). We do not find the word *Upanayana* at all in the *Rigveda.* There is the word *Brahmacārin* occurring once in the *Rigveda.* In the books that have already been written on the subject of education in ancient India, it has been uniformly said that the word *Brahmacārin* means the boy initiated into the learning of the *Vedas.* The passage in the *Rigveda* is:

> The *Brahmacārin* goes engaged in duty; he is a member of the body of the gods.[1]
>
> (Rigveda X-109-5)

For this hymn, the author (*Ṛṣi*) is a *Brahmavādinī* (one who discourses on *Brahman*), named Juhū. From this itself we can understand that it is a very mystic hymn; I must confess that the sense is very obscure. Even the name of the author is not definite according to tradition. Ūrdhvanābhā, son of Brahmā is also given as the author, as an alternative. Thus the *Sarvānukramaṇī*[2] gives the author etc., in the passage:

[1] ब्रह्मचारी चरति वेविषद्विषः स देवानां भवत्येकमङ्गम् ।

Sarvānukramaṇī gives the index of all details, like the author, the metre and the deity of the hymns.

te 'avadan,[1] seven, Juhū wife of Brahmā, or Ūrdhvanābhā son of Brahmā.[2]

Sāyaṇa gives the meaning of the *Rigvedic* passage cited above as:

Oh gods formerly he wandered about as a *Brahmacārin*, *i.e.*, as a bachelor, since he had no wife[3].

From the whole spirit of the passage, we find that there is no reference to the boy-initiate in the hymn at all. The reference seems to be to some one who was devoted to the deeper contemplation of the nature of *Brahman*; but Sāyaṇa takes the word *Brahmacārin* in its secondary significance of a bachelor or celebate. The *Rigvedic* tradition refers to two sorts of people, the *Ṛṣis* who knew the nature of the gods and who composed the hymns in praise of such gods, perhaps who were also engaged in the sacrifices, and the *Brahmacārins* who thought about the deeper problems of the reality of the universe. Thus Skandasvāmin cites a story where Arcanānas of the Family of Atri officiated as priest at the sacrifice of a king named Rathavīti. Arcanānas had a son named S'yāvās'va who was a *Brahmacārin*. Once he went to the king being invited for the performance of the sacrifice, along with his son. At the end of the sacrifice, he met the daughter of the king who was unmarried and sought her hand for his son. After consulting his queen, he replied

[1] This is the beginning of the hymn.

[2] तेऽवदन् सप्त जुहूर्ब्रह्मजाया ब्राह्मो वोर्ध्वनाभा.

[3] हे देवा: पूर्वं स ब्रह्मचारी जायाभावेन ब्रह्मचारी चरति ।

that they had never a son-in-law who was not a *Ṛṣi* and that his son S'yāvās'va was only a *Brahmacārin* and not an *Ṛṣi.*[1] Here evidently the disqualification was not that the youth was a boy-initiate or that he was a bachelor but that he could not have the vision of gods (*Ṛṣi*) and was devoted to *Brahman* knowledge (*Brahmacārin*).

From the mere appearance of the word *Brahmacārin* we cannot say that there is also a reference to *Upanayana* and *Brahmacaryās'rama* (stage of studentship). I am not denying the existence of such institutions in the *Rigvedic* age; what I am doing is only to say that the word *Brahmacārin* in the *Rigveda* passage cited above is no authority for the establishment of the existence of such institutions at that time.

There are two hymns in the *Atharvaveda* where there is a definite description of a *Brahmacārin.* The first is a small hymn of five verses, where there is the reference to the process of making the *Brahmacārin* impotent, as a step to his being able to devote his whole attention to the acquisition of the *Brahman* knowledge, without being distracted by considerations of the world and its enjoyments. The first verse in the hymn is:

> Oh plant, thy fame is spread abroad as best of all the herbs that grow; make this man today a eunuch that he may wear the horn of hair.[2]
>
> (Atharvaveda VI-138-1)

[1] Com. on *Rigveda* V. 61. 1.

[2] त्वं वीरुधां श्रेष्ठतमाभिश्रुतास्योषधे ।
इमं मे अद्य पुरुषं क्लीबमोपशिनं कृधि ॥

The same idea more or less continues in the whole hymn. Is this the idea that is fitting for a boy of eight years who is to enter the stage of studenthship? Or is it more fitting for a man of advanced age who desires to retire from the affairs of the world and enter the stage of what may be called *Saṁnyāsa* (renunciation)? The matter becomes clearer when we consider the next hymn relating to a *Brahmacārin* in the *Atharvaveda.* This is a fairly long hymn of 26 verses. The dress and other details of a *Brahmacārin* are described in this hymn. Take the verse:

> With a lighted fuel goes the *Brahmacārin*, clad in black buck-skin, consecrate, long-bearded.[1]
>
> (Atharvaveda XI-5-6)

Here there is a specific mention of long beards, which is an impossibility for a boy entering the stage of studentship. Therefore the mention of the word *Brahmacārin* does not mean that this suggests *Upanayana* (initiation to study) etc. Here the *Brahmacārin* meant is one who discards the world and enters the stage of *Vānaprastha* (life in the forest hermitage) devoting his whole time to the consideration of the problem of *Brahman.*

I had to enter into this long discussion only in so far as scholars who have written books on the subject have said that these references relate to the student

[1] ब्रह्मचार्येति समिधा समिद्धः
कार्ष्णं वसानो दीक्षितो दीर्घश्मश्रुः ॥

after *Upanayana* (initiation).[1] Really I have not been able to find any reference to *Upanayana* in the Vedic *Saṁhitās* (original texts). The words *Upanayana* and *Upanīta* appear in the *Rigveda*; but they mean only "to bring near" in the ordinary sense without the special meaning of "initiation", bringing the boy near the teacher for study. But reference in the hymn on frogs in the *Rigveda*, to the student repeating the words of the teacher is clear enough regarding the particular type of teaching that was associated with the *Upanayana* ceremony.[2]

It has been held by some[3] that the passage in the *Rigveda*:

Young, with fine robes and covered around.[4]

(III-8-4)

[1] History of *Dharma Śāstra* by MM. P. V. Kane, Vol. II, pp. 268 and 270.

[2] This idea is found in the *Rāmāyaṇa* of Kambar in Tamil.

Kalviyiṟṟigal kaṇakkāyar kambalai
Palviḍac-cirārenap-pakarva pallari
Cellidattalatonrutaittal ceykalā
Nallaṟi vālarin avinda nāvelām

Kiṣkindhakāṇḍa, Kārkālapaṭalam (Description of rainy season), 115.

Frogs of many species croak like the noisy boys of many grades with their learned teacher. They were silent like the good wise men who utter not anything except where acceptable.

I am indebted to Sri T. P. Palaniappa Pillai, B.O.L., Reader in Tamil, Sri Venkateswara Oriental Research Institute, Tirupati for this parallelism.

[3] History of *Dharma Śāstra* by MM. P. V. Kane, Vol. II, p. 269.

[4] युवा सुवासाः परिवीतः

describing a sacrificial pole (*Yūpa*), has reference to the robes of a *Brahmacārin.* It will be more appropriate if the description has reference to a citizen in fine robes, and not to a *Brahmacārin* in his garment and girdle. The expression "covered around" (*Parivīta*) may refer to the fine robes, or it may be a second robe on the upper part of the body. I do not accept this as an allusion to *Brahmacarya.*

The same continuity and unity of tradition which we are able to trace between the *Rigveda* and the *Āraṇyaka* literature are found existing between the *Brāhmaṇa* (including the *Āraṇayaka*) literature and the later texts relating to the various sacraments, the *Gṛhyasūtras* and the *Dharmasūtras*, forming parts of the *Kalpasūtras* which form one among the six *Vedāngas* (accessory texts for *Vedic* study). We do not know when these *Kalpasūtras* were written ; but we know that the system has not undergone any change from those days when the *Kalpasūtras* were written up to the very recent times. The same *Upanayana* ceremony, the same system of teaching the proper recitation of the *Vedas*, continued in an unbroken tradition for at least twenty-five centuries from the age of the *Kalpasūtras* to the present day. If we are able to trace a system for so many centuries up to our own days, there is no reason for doubting its continuity backwards also for innumerable centuries. Assisted by this single indirect allusion to the system of reciting the *Vedas* by a student after his teacher, we are justified in assuming that the *Upanayana* ceremony and the system of studying the *Vedas* by rote from a teacher was a *Rigvedic*, and perhaps an eaven earlier, institution. What I want to emphasise is that the passages:

> When among them one repeats the words of the other like a student that of the teacher.[1]
>
> (*Rigveda* VII-103-5)

is identical in purport to the passage in the *Taittirīyāraṇyaka*:

> One should study what has been prescribed for his own study[2]

and the *Kalpasūtra* passage:

> Study the Vedas remaining under the control of the teacher.[3] (Āśv. Gṛhya-Sūtra I-22-2)

It has been made out by those who have written on this subject that the original system of *Upanayana* must have been a very simple one and that the elaborate ceremonial found in the later literature must have gradually developed.[4]

The fact is that scholars who have written on this subject have not made any distinction between *Upanayana* (initiation) and *Upasadana* (approach to the teacher). The former is the ceremony of a student being initiated to the Vedic study under the teacher;

[1] Already cited on p. 5.

[2] Already cited on p. 5.

[3] आचार्याधीनो वेदमधीष्वा

[4] History of *Dharma Sāstra* by MM. P. V. Kane, Vol. II, p. 273.

and this is done by the parent. Then there is the latter, namely, *Upasadana*, which is a voluntary approach to a great teacher by an advanced student for further study. Here there is no special ceremony prescribed. In the *Upaniṣads* we come across various incidents of students going to great teachers in search of higher knowledge. This aspect will be considered again later. Here I propose to take into consideration only the question of *Upanayana* and the study of the *Vedas* thereafter.

III. SVĀDHYAYĀDHYAYANA

The *Upanayana* ceremony is to be performed in the eighth year for a Brahmin, in the eleventh year for a Kshatriya and in the twelfth year for a Vaisya. The ceremony is described in the *Ās'valāyana-Gṛhya-Sūtra*[1] in *Kaṇḍikās* 19 to 21 in the first Chapter. Then in the twenty-second *Kaṇḍikā* the duties of a *Brahmacarin* are described. Texts are all fairly uniform in the matter of the details of the *Upanayana* ceremony. The ages prescribed for the ceremony for the various castes is either after birth or from the time of pregnancy. Thus we have the Sūtra :

> One shall initiate a Brahmin in the eighth year ; or in the eighth year from pregnancy ; a Kshatriya in the eleventh ; a Vaisya in the twelfth.[2]
>
> (Ās'v. Gṛhya Sūtras 1-19-1 to 4)

[1] The reference is to the edition in the Adyar Library Series No. 44.

[2] अष्टमे वर्षे ब्राह्मणमुपनयेत् । गर्भाष्टमे वा । एकादशे क्षत्रियम् । द्वादशे वैश्यम् ।

This is not the latest age at which the *Upanayana* shall be performed; the ceremony can be postponed up to 16, 22 and 24 respectively for the three castes. Thus it is said:

> The time does not elapse for a Brahmin till the sixteenth year; for a Kshatriya till the twenty-second; for a Vaisya till the twenty-fourth.[1]
>
> (Ās'v. Gṛhya-Sūtra I-19-5 and 6)

If a boy is not initiated into study at this age, there is social penalty. It is said:

> After this, they have the *Sāvitrī*[2] fallen off; one shall not initiate them, one shall not teach them, one shall not associate with them in sacrifices and one shall not have social dealings with them.[3]
>
> (Ās'v. Gṛhya-Sūtra I-19, 6 and 7)

One may consider why there is this difference among the various castes regarding the age of *Upanayana*. The differentiation is not merely in the matter of the age prescribed for *Upanayana*. It is also in a variety of other details. Regarding the robes to be worn by a *Brahmacārin*, it is said:

> The boy who wears ornaments, whose (hair on the) head is arranged properly, who wears a garment that has not been washed (*i.e.*, a new garment)

[1] आ षोडशात् ब्राह्मणस्यानतीत: काल: । आ द्वाविंशात् क्षत्रियस्य । आ चतुर्विंशाद्वैश्यस्य ।

[2] Sāvitri is Gāyatrī.

[3] अत ऊर्ध्वं पतितसावित्रीका भवन्ति । नैनानुपनयेन्नाध्यापयेन्न याजयेन्नैभि-र्व्यवहरेयुः ।

or an antelope's skin if he is a Brahmin, the skin of a spotted dear if he is a Kshatriya, or a goat's skin if he is a Vaisya.[1] (Ās'v. Gṛhya-Sūtra I-19-8)

If they wear garments, they must wear garments that are dyed ; a Brahmin shall wear reddish yellow one, a Kshatriya shall wear a light reddish one, the Vaisya a yellow one.[2] (Ās'v. Gṛhya-Sūtra 1-19-9)

About *Mekhalā* (girdle) there is the prescription :

One made of *Muñja* grass for a Brahmin, one made of a bow-string for a Kshatriya, one made of wool for a Vaisya.[3] (Ās'v. Gṛhya-Sūtra I-19-11)

The stick that they wear are also different as :

One made of *Palās'a* for a Brahmin, one made of *Udumbara* tree for a Kshatriya, one made of *Bilva*[4] tree for a Vaisya ; one reaching up to the tuft of hair for a Brahmin, one reaching up to the forehead for a Kshatriya, one reaching up to the heart for a Vaisya.[5]
(Ās'v. Gṛhya-Sūtra I-19-13)

[1] अलंकृतं कुमारं कुशलीकृतशिरसमहतेन वाससा संवीतमैणेयेन वाजिनेन ब्राह्मणं रौरवेण क्षत्रियमाजेन वैश्यम् ।

[2] यदि वासांसि वसीरन् रक्तानि वसीरन् काषायं ब्राह्मणो माञ्जिष्ठं क्षत्रियो हारिद्रं वैश्यः ।

[3] मौञ्जी ब्राह्मणस्य धनुर्ज्या क्षत्रियस्य आवी वैश्यस्य ।

[4] These are three kinds of trees.

[5] पालाशो ब्राह्मणस्य । औदुम्बरः क्षत्रियस्य । बैल्वो वैश्यस्य । केशसंमितो ब्राह्मणस्य । ललाटसंमितः क्षत्रियस्य । प्राणसंमितो वैश्यस्य ।

After this follows the general statement:

everything for everyone.[1] (Āsv. Gṛhy-Sūtra I-20-1)

This choice, according to the commentators is only with reference to the stick and have no reference to the garment and the girdle:

All kinds of sticks for all can be as alternatives.[2] (Com. of Devasvāmin on the above)

I will try to consider presently that this option must be the survival of an age when there was no such distinction made on a community basis.

But let us now consider how such distinctions are explained. It cannot be that according to Indian tradition, Brahmins have better intellect than Kshatriyas and Vaisyas. In the *Upaniṣads*, the intellectual emiminence of the Kshatriyas has been fully vindicated. There is a very mechanical explanation given, namely, that the *Mantra* (the Vedic passage) imparted to a Brahmin at the *Upanayana* is in the *Gāyatrī* metre with eight syllables a line, while the *Mantras* imparted to a Kshatriya and a Vaisya at that same ceremony are in the *Tṛṣṭup* and *Jagatī* metres with eleven and twelve syllables a line. The age for the *Upanayana* has been determined by these numbers. This difference in the metres of the *Mantras* imparted to the students of the three castes is found in some *Gṛhya-Sūtras* as follows:

1 सर्वे वा सर्वेषाम्.

2 सर्वे वा दण्डाः सर्वेषां विकल्पेन भवन्ति.

Let him recite a *Gāyatrī* to a Brahmin, a *Tṛṣṭup* to a Kshatriya, a *Jagatī* to a Vais'ya.[1]

(Sāṅkhyāyana Gṛhya-Sūtra II-5-4 to 6)

In the next *Sūtra* there is an option :

But let it be, anyhow, a verse sacred to Savitar.[2]

(Sāṅkh-Gṛhya-Sūtra II-5-7)

This choice is made clearer in the *Pāraskara-Gṛhya-Sūtra* :

Or a *Gāyatrī* to all.[3] (II-3-10)

The previous specifications for the three castes are identical with what is given in the *Sāṅkhyāyana-Gṛhya-Sūtra*. This explanation based on the number of syllables must be a later exhibition of dry intellectualism. This option must again be a survival of a condition when such distinctions were not made on a community basis.

The true fact must be that these prescriptions have become confined to Brahmins in course of time. We do not find any such differentiation in the earlier stages in the Vedic literature. I will explain the true position. The age at which the study is to terminate is not quite clear. The *Ās'valāyana-Gṛhya-Sūtra* says that the study should be for twelve years, or until the study is finished. This latter option seems to be for those who could finish the study earlier.

[1] गायत्रीं ब्राह्मणायानुब्रूयात् । त्रिष्टुभं क्षत्रियाय । जगतीं वैश्याय ।

[2] सावित्रीं त्वेव वा ।

[3] सर्वेषां वा गायत्रीम् ।

The studentship for the *Veda* is for twelve years; or it may be till the study is over.[1]

(Ās'v. Gṛhya-Sūtra I-22-3 and 4)

This period is also found in some other texts. In some texts it is said that the student can remain in the household of the teacher studying the *Vedas* for forty-eight years, devoting twelve years for each *Veda*. That means that he should remain a *Brahmacārin* till he is fifty-six years old if a Brahmin, fifty-nine if a Kshatriya and sixty if a Vaisya. This is an impossibility; that is not the fit age for the ceremonial "bath" (*snāna*) marking the termination of study and for marriage which should follow the study.

At a time when intensive study of the *Vedas* was confined to the Brahmins, and when such study remained as a mere ceremonial among the other two castes, it was sufficient if the boys of the other two castes started their course later. Although the prescription of the "study of what has been prescribed for one's own study" (*Svādhyāyādhyayana*) was common to the boys of the three castes in the beginning, this education with a view to acquiring a knowledge of the *Vedas* as fit to be used in the sacrifices became confined to the Brahmins at a later stage. Therefore the purely secular education of the prior stage must have been continued for a longer time among the two other castes, and the Brahmins alone had their *Upanayana* at the age of eight. This may be the

[1] द्वादशवर्षाणि वेदब्रह्मचर्यम् । ग्रहणान्तं वा ।

explanation for the differences in the age at which *Vedic* study was started among the various castes.

Although the age at which the *Upanayana* should be performed is definitely fixed, the age at which the study could be terminated is not so rigidly determined. As I have already said, the usual period of study lasts for twelve years. But there is the option of terminating the study when the student is able to finish the entire prescribed course of study in a lesser time.

Even in regard to this period of twelve years as the normal period of study for a student, there is a difference of opinion. Does it include or exclude items like *Mahānāmnī*? Some hold that the ceremonial called *Godāna* [1] should be performed sixteen years after *Upanayana* or in the sixteenth year after birth. In this case, it will work out as follows. If the twelve years do not include the *Mahānāmnī*, there would be twelve years for the study of the *Veda* and then three years for *Mahānāmnī*; and the whole course will end in the sixteenth year. The texts prescribe the *Godāna* for the sixteenth year after birth, that is eight years after *Upanayana*. There is left a period of four years after the *Godāna*. This can be the period for the *Mahānāmnī*.

The two views regarding the *Mahānāmni* are given by Devasvāmin in his commentary on the *Āśvalāyana-Gṛhya-Sūtra* as follows:

There shall be twelve years for the studentship for *Veda*. Now why is the word *Veda* given here?

[1] These two terms will be explained later.

It is to indicate that this time is only for the ceremony connected with the *Veda*. Therefore the application of *Mahānāmnī* etc. comes after the twelve years. This being so, the *Godāna* shall be sixteen years after *Upanayana*. This idea is established from the use of the word *Veda*. Otherwise there need not have been the use of the word *Veda*. This is the opinion of some. Others say as follows: *Godāna* comes in the sixteenth year after birth, which is included even within the twelve years, being included in it. There may be no separation of *Mahānāmnī* etc. either. Why? Because *Mahānāmnīs* are a part of the Veda. Therefore, this specification of time is along with these (*Mahānāmnīs* etc.).[1]

(Devasvāmin's com. on I-22-3)

Those who complete their studies and perform the ceremonial bath are classified in three groups. The commentator Devasvāmin puts it thus:

When the Teacher (Ās'valāyana) says so (*i.e.*, till the study is over), there has been indicated three kinds of baths, study bath, observance bath and study-cum-observance bath. He who observed *Brahmacarya*

[1] द्वादशवर्षाणि वेदब्रह्मचर्यं वेदस्य ब्रह्मचर्यं भवति। अथ वेदग्रहणं किमर्थं क्रियते। कथं वेदव्रतस्यैवायं कालनियमः स्यादिति। तेन महानाम्निकादीनां ऊर्ध्वं द्वादशेभ्यः प्रयोगः। एवं च कृत्वा उपनयनात् प्रभृति षोडशे वर्षे गोदानं भवति। वेदग्रहणादयमर्थः साध्यते। इतरथा हि वेदग्रहणमेव नाकरिष्यत्। एवमेके। अन्ये—जन्मनः प्रभृति षोडशे वर्षे गोदानं द्वादशेष्वेव वर्षेष्वन्तर्भूतं तन्मध्यपातित्वात्। माहानाम्नींनां वापृथग्भावः। कस्मात्। महानाम्नीनां वेदैकदेशत्वात्। तस्मात् सहैवैतैः कालनियमोऽयम्।

for twelve years and completed his study and bathes, is called one who has performed the study-cum-observance bath. He who even before twelve years completed the study and bathes is called one who has performed study bath. He, on the other hand, who observed *Brahmacarya* for twelve years but could not complete his studies and then bathes, is called one who has performed the observance bath.[1]

(Devasvāmin's com. on Ās'va Gṛhya-Sūtra I-22-4)

There are thus three kinds of students who finish their study. Some are able to complete their whole study before the lapse of the prescribed period of twelve years; some are able to finish the study within that prescribed period; there are still others (perhaps only a small minority) who are not able to complete the study during that period (they could only observe the ceremonials). The last set give up a part of their course. There are two parts in the course, one part that is obligatory and another part that is left to the choice of the student. Thus says the commentator:

But he (who could not finish the whole course within the prescribed period) gives up a part of the study and bathes. The study is of two kinds, one to be done in the village and the other in the forest.

[1] एवं च कुर्वताचार्येण त्रिविधं स्नानं दर्शितं भवति—विद्यास्नानं व्रतस्नानं विद्याव्रतस्नानं इति। यो द्वादशवर्षाणि ब्रह्मचर्यं कृत्वा अधीतविद्यः स्नानं करोति असौ विद्याव्रतस्नातकः। यः प्राग्द्वादशवर्षेभ्यो विद्यामधीत्य स्नानं करोति असौ विद्यास्नातकः। यः पुनर्द्वादशवर्षाणि ब्रह्मचर्यं कृत्वा अनधीतविद्यः स व्रतस्नातकः।

> Among them, the study of *Mahānāmnīs* is obligatory, what are called studies in the forest. He who without acquiring this study, does his bath, though he has acquired various other studies, does not become one who has performed the bath. It is possible to give up the study to be done in the village.[1]

We come to this position. Even at present, we have some sort of classification of students who have completed their studies. Some sort of classification existed even in those early days. The clever students could complete their studies in lesser time than is prescribed. The average students completed their course within the prescribed period. A few could not finish the course within the prescribed period. They give up a part of their course.

This shows that the students could not stay at the household of the teacher for a period longer than what has been prescribed. There is no option left to have the whole course finished in a longer period. The question has to be considered why it is that there is a prescription for the student to stay in the household of the teacher for periods of twelve years for each of the *Vedas*, totalling forty-eight years for the four *Vedas*, while there is no provision for a student to stay in the teacher's household for a longer period than twelve

[1] स तु कांचिद्विद्यामुत्सृज्य स्नानं करोति। ग्राम्या आरण्या इत्युभयलक्षणा च विद्या भवति। तत्र च महानाम्नीनां नित्यानामध्ययनम्। यां पुनरारण्यां ब्रुवते योऽनधीत्यैतां विद्यां अधीयमानोऽपि बह्वीं विद्यां स्नानं करोति स स्नातको न भवति। ग्राम्यां तूत्स्रष्टुं विद्यां शक्यम्।

years to complete his full course when he is not able to complete it within the twelve years prescribed. When I mentioned the provision for the study of the four *Vedas* during forty-eight years, I expressed some doubt about its genuineness and authenticity. The position must be that the students had to finish their study within this period of twelve years, and those who could not do it were not fit to have the complete course of study. They had to be satisfied with having stayed at the household of the teacher performing all the prescribed ceremonials.

In the matter of the classification, there is a great difference between the ancient system and the modern system. In the old system, whatever part was finished was finished completely, and a part was omitted. At present the system is that all follow the same course, but one could satisfy the needs of education, even if his knowledge is partial, even if he acquires only a certain percentage of the whole knowledge.

IV. Elementary Education

The *Upanayana* is not the first start of the study by a boy. The *Upanayana* is only the start of the *Vedic* study. There must have been some course of studies of an elementary nature prior to the *Upanayana.* There is no evidence of any such initiation to this first study as a *Saṁskāra* (sacrament). After the birth of a boy and prior to his *Upanayana*, the only sacraments are *Jātakarma* (first purification after birth), *Nāmkaraṇa* (naming the boy), *Annaprāśana* (first feeding) and *Cūḍākarma* (first shaving the hair and formation of the tuft).

There is a view that at some distant past, there was no need for a preliminary study prior to the *Upanayana* and the start of the *Vedic* studies. The *Upanayana* must have been regularised at such a time. At that time, there was no alphabet known to Indians and there was no grammar also to be learned by the boys. This is a view that has been expressed by some scholars.[1]

It is true that there is no mention of a sacrament to mark the first initiation of a boy to writing and reading, except in very recent texts. As matters stand at present, there are two ceremonies performed, one to initiate the boy to write and the second to initiate him to read. The former is more elaborate; in the latter, there is no real religious ceremony attached. But both are now practised, and as separate ceremonies.

I am not at all sure whether the absence of a mention of a ceremony for the first start of the education of a boy, prior to *Upanayana* and *Vedic* study, as a separate sacrament in the texts, is due to the absence of the art of writing and of a grammar to be taught at that time. There are many things which a boy learns in childhood, and every one of them is not associated with a sacrament. The child learns to sit up, to move about, to walk, to swim and so on. There are no sacraments associated with these events in his life.

[1] See Dr. A. S. Altekar, *Education in Ancient India*, 1934, p. 3.

But there is the ceremony called *Niṣkramaṇa* (moving out of the house) described in the texts; and this is such a simple event. Similarly, even in the matter of education, certain aspects that have a deeper significance are associated with sacraments. This may be the case with *Upanayana*, while there is no sacrament associated with the first initiation into writing and reading. They are done as a matter of course after the *Cūḍākarma* and before the *Upanayana*. Kālidāsa says about Raghu:

> He with his *Cūḍākarma* finished and joined along with the sons of ministers of the same age wearing flowing sets of front tufts, entered the whole literature through the proper study of the alphabet, just as one would reach the ocean through the mouth of a river.[1]
>
> (*Raghuvaṁśa* III-28)

In commenting upon this, Mallinātha cites a passage:

> But when he has attained the fifth year, one shall have his first initiation to study performed.[2]

About the *Cūḍākarma*, Manu says:

> Even for all the Twice-born, the *Cūḍākarma* must be performed according to rules; it has to be done in the first year or in the third, as has been prescribed in the Vedas.[3] (II-35)

[1] स वृत्तचूडश्चलकाकपक्षकैरमात्यपुत्रैः सवयोभिरन्वितः ।
लिपेर्यथावद्ग्रहणेन वाङ्मयं नदीमुखेनेव समुद्रमाविशत् ॥

[2] प्राप्ते तु पञ्चमे वर्षे विद्यारम्भं च कारयेत् ।

[3] चूडा कार्या द्विजातीनां सर्वेषामेव धर्मतः ।
प्रथमेऽब्दे तृतीये वा कर्तव्या श्रुतिचोदनात ॥

Ās'valāyana prescribes the *Cūḍākarma* in the third year:

> Caula in the third year; or according to the Law of the family.[1] (Ās'v. Gṛhya-Sūtra I-17-1)

Sāṅkhyāyana-Gṛhya-Sūtra has it at the end of the first year, or in the third year. It is in the fifth year for the Kshatriyas and in the seventh for Vaisyas.[2] *Pāraskara-Gṛhya-Sūtra* prescribes *Cuḍākarma* at the end of the first year or before the lapse of the third year.[3] It cannot therefore be that the *Cuḍākarma* is immediately followed by the first initiation to the study of writing and reading.

In the *Uttararāmacarita* of *Bhavabhūti*, it is said that Kus'a and Lava, the sons of S'rī Rāma, had their *Cūḍākarma* performed and their education started. Ātreyi who could not continue the study at the hermitage of Vālmīki, where the sons of S'rī Rāma were brought up, in so far as she was surpassed in intellectual capacity by these two boys, says to the Vanadevatā (forest nymph):

> But they, being adopted by the great Vālmīki through the responsibility of bringing them up, were protected by him. For them whose *Cūḍākarma* was

[1] तृतीये वर्षे चौळम् । यथा कुलधर्मं वा ।

[2] संवत्सरे चूडाकर्म । तृतीये वा वर्षे । पञ्चमे क्षत्रियस्य । सप्तमे वैश्यस्य (I, 28. 1 to 4).

[3] सांवत्सरिकस्य चूडाकरणम् । तृतीये वाप्रतिहते (II. 1. 1, 12).

> performed, the three-fold studies, avoiding the three-fold (*Veda*) were well taught.[1] (Act II)

All that we can say from this is that the first initiation into writing and reading was performed after *Cūḍākarma* and prior to *Upanayana*. Three years is too early an age for a boy to start practice of writing and reading. It may be said that for Kshatriyas, the age for *Cūḍākarma* is five, and, as such, the first initiation into writing and reading can follow the *Cūḍākarma* immediately. If it is so, it is only a chance coincidence and not a rule. It is not said, as some scholars have asserted,[2] that the education of a prince should commence at the time of the *Cūḍākarma*, and for this the *Arthaśāstra* of Kauṭilya has been cited as authority. But the *Arthaśāstra* makes no such prescription. All that is said in that text is:

> Sciences shall be studied and their precepts strictly observed under the authority of specialists teachers; having undergone the ceremony of tonsure, the student shall learn the alphabet and arithmetic. After the sacramental initiation, he shall study the Triple *Vedas* and the science of logic under proper authorities, economics under Heads of Departments, and the science of Government under

[1] तौ तु भगवता वाल्मीकिना धात्रीकर्मतः परिगृह्य पोषितौ रक्षितौ च । निवृत्त-चौळकर्मणोस्तयोस्त्रयीवर्जमितरास्तिस्रो विद्याः सावधानेन परिनिष्ठापिताः ।

[2] Dr. A. S. Altekar, *Education in Ancient India*, 1935. p. 4.

politicians who have both theoretical and practical knowledge.[1]

Here it would be found that Kālidāsa is practically reproducing the words of the *Arthas'āstra*, and Bhavabhūti says that Kus'a and Lava were at that stage taught only the three subjects of study, outside the three-fold *Veda*. The three-fold *Veda* is to be taught only after *Upanayana*. Vīrarāghava in his commentary on the above passage in the *Uttararāmacarita* says that the three subjects taught were *Āyurveda*, *Dhanurveda* and *Gāndharvaveda* (medicine, archery and music). Putting the *Arthas'āstra*, the *Raghuvaṁs'a* and the *Uttararāmacarita* together, we find that after *Cūḍākarma* and prior to the *Upanayana*, there must have been some education imparted to the boys, which consisted of writing and reading, elements of grammar, literature and a few *S'āstras*. *Vedic* study along with the *Vedāṅgas* started only after the *Upanayana*.

From the details of the *Upanayana* ceremony and from the duties prescribed for a student after the *Upanayana*, it is certain that the boy must have been having some previous education, which might have consisted mainly of language and literature and a few *S'āstras*, besides the practice in writing and reading. Thus we find that there are two stages in the education of a child; first there is the elementary education at

[1] विद्यानां तु यथास्वमाचार्यप्रामाण्याद्विनयो नियमश्च । वृत्तचौलकर्मा लिपिं संख्यानं चोपयुञ्जीत । वृत्तोपनयनस्त्रयीमान्वीक्षिकीं च शिष्टेभ्यो वार्तामध्यक्षेभ्यो दण्डनीतिं वक्तृप्रयोक्तृभ्यः (P. 10 in Mysore Ed. 1909).

home, consisting of practice in writing and reading, language and literature and a few *S'āstras*; then there is the *Upanayana* and the study of the *Vedas*. This study of the *Vedas* along with the *Vedāṅgas* after the *Upanayana*, is obligatory; and as preparatory to this obligatory *Vedic* study, the elementary education at home prior to the *Upanayana* must also be taken as obligatory.

V. Brāhmaṇas

This obligatory study, usually styled *Svādhyāyādhyayana* (study of what has been prescribed for one's own study) has been glorified in the *Taittirīyāraṇyaka* and in the *S'atapatha-Brāhmaṇa*. The second *Prapāṭhaka* (Book) of the *Taittirīyāraṇyaka* starts with a description of the *Yajñopavīta* (the sacred thread worn by the "Twice-born", which is necessary for the study of the Vedas):

> Therefore one with a sacred thread alone shall study, shall minister at sacrifices, shall sacrifice, for the proper process of the sacrifice.[1]

There is also prescribed the skin and the garment, which too are found in the *Gṛhya-Sūtras*.

> wearing on the right side a skin or a garment[2]

Then in the second *Anuvāka* (Chapter) the morning, noon and evening oblutions (*Sandhyāvandana*) is glorified. It is in the fifteenth *Anuvāka* that the *Svādhyāyādhyayana* (the study of what has prescribed

[1] तस्माद्यज्ञोपवीत्येवाधीयीत याजयेद्यजेत वा यज्ञस्य प्रसृत्यै ।

[2] आजिनं वासो वा दक्षिणत उपवीय ।

for one's own study) has been formally enjoined. The passage is:

> Therefore what has been prescribed for one's own study should be studied; and that sacrifice which one studies, through that and that there accrues one's desires; there comes about union with Fire, Wind, Sun.[1]

Prior to this, various details are given like the five great sacrifices (*Mahāyajñas*) of which the recitation of the *Veda* (*Brahmayajña*) is one. There is also described the days proper for study and the days on which there shall be no study. In the case of the recitation of the *Vedas*, it is said that the study should be in the forest.

> One who proposes to sacrifice with the recitation of the *Vedas* shall first sip water three times, going to the eastern direction, at a distance from the village from whence one cannot see the roof of the village house[2], facing the north or the north-east, when the sun rises, wearing the garment on the right side, sitting, keeping the hands washed; then he shall wipe the face twice, once touch the head, the eyes, the nose, the ears, the heart.[3] (II-11)

[1] तस्मात् स्वाध्यायोऽध्येतव्यो यं यं क्रतुमधीते तेन तेनास्येष्टं भवत्यग्नेर्वायोरादित्यस्य सायुज्यं गच्छति ।

[2] This is what is meant by the term अच्छदिर्दर्शे ; Sāyaṇa gives that explanation—गृहस्योपर्याच्छादनार्थानि तृणकटादीनि छर्दींषि। यावति दूरे तानि न दृश्यन्ते तावद्दूरमच्छदिर्दर्शम् । तत्र गत्वा ।

[3] ब्रह्मयज्ञेन यक्ष्यमाणः प्राच्यां दिशि ग्रामादच्छदिर्दर्श उदीच्यां प्रागुदीच्यां वोदित आदित्ये दक्षिणत उपवीयोपविश्य हस्ताववनिज्य त्रिराचामेद्द्विः परिमृज्य सकृदुपस्पृश्य शिरश्चक्षुषी नासिके श्रोत्रे हृदयमालभ्य ।

In the case of such students who cannot conform to this prescription strictly, there are certain restrictions allowed.

> One may study what has been prescribed for one's own study in the village, in his mind, either by day or at night . . . either one who is incapable of doing it in the forest, or of doing it with muttering. One shall certainly study what is prescribed for one's own study, standing or walking, or sitting, or lying down; that person who knowing thus performs the penance and who studies what has been prescribed for one's own study, shall become holy [1] (II-12).

In the first of the two citations above, one will note some similarity with the words found in the *Gṛhya-Sūtras*.

In the *S'atapatha Brāhmaṇa* also there is a section relating to *Brahmacārin* and the *Svādhyāyādhyayana*. Just as we saw even in the *Taittirīyāraṇyaka* certain traces of the *Upanayana* and the *Brahmacarya* found described in the later Texts, relating to *Yajñopavīta*, *Ajina* (skin), *Vastra* (garment), so in the *S'atapatha-Brāhmaṇa* too, we find similar traces of the ceremony described in the later Texts. Thus there is the passage:

> He says "Thou are a *Brahmacārin*" . . . "sip water" . . . "Perform the rites".[2]
>
> (S'at-Path. Br. XI-5-4-5)

[1] ग्रामे मनसा स्वाध्यायमधीयीत दिवा नक्तं वा . . . . उतारण्येऽबल उत वाचोततिष्ठन्नुत व्रजन्नुतासीन उत शयान: अधीयीतैव स्वाध्यायं तपस्वी पुण्यो भवति य एवं विद्वान् स्वाध्यायमधीते ।

[2] ब्रह्मचार्यसीत्याह . . . अपोऽशानेति . . . कर्म कुर्विति ।

Following this there are the restrictions in the life of *Brahmacārin* that are also mentioned in the later Texts :

> When one has admitted a Brahmin as a *Brahmacārin*, he shall not carry on sexual intercourse.[1]
>
> (S'at-Path-Br-XI-5-4-16)

and

> When one becomes a *Brahmacārin*, one shall not drink alcohol.[2]
>
> (S'at-Path-Br-XI-5-4-18)

There are also passages prescribing *Svādhyāyādhyayana* in this portion of the *S'atapatha-Brāhmaṇa*.

> Now then the glorification of the study of what has been prescribed for one's own study.[3]
>
> (S'at-Path-Br-XI-5-7-1)

This is the opening section. Then at the end of each of the succeeding three sections there is the passage repeated :

> Therefore what has been prescribed for one's own study shall be studied[4].

This is followed by the passages :

> The *Ṛks* verily are honey ; the *Sāmans* are ghee ; the *Yajus* are nectar.[5] (section 5)

[1] न ब्राह्मणं ब्रह्मचर्यमुपनीय मिथुनं चरेत् ।

[2] न ब्रह्मचारी सन् मध्वश्नीयात् ।

[3] अथातः स्वाध्यायप्रशंसा ।

[4] तस्मात् स्वाध्यायोऽध्येतव्यः ।

[5] मधु ह वा ऋचः । घृतं सामानि । अमृतं यजूंषि ।

> He verily propitiates the gods with honey; for him who knowing the *Ṛks* as this, studies day by day what is prescribed for his own study, they, being propitiated, satisfies with all desires, all enjoyments[1] (Section 6)

There are similar statements about *Sāman*[2] and *Yajus*[3] in the next two sections, and about dialogues, mythologies and ancient legends in the next one.[4] Then follows the final statement:

> Verily, just as these Deites have not moved and have not performed (rites), even so will the Brahmin be on that day on which he does not study what is prescribed for his own study; therefore what is prescribed for one's own study shall be studied; hence at least let him recite either the *Ṛks*, or the *Sāmans*, or the songs[5] or the prescriptive passage,[6] to ensure the specification of the rites.[7] (Section 10)

[1] मधुना ह वा एष देवांस्तर्पयति । य एवं विद्वानृचोऽहरहः स्वाध्यायमधीते त एनं तृप्तास्तर्पयन्ति सर्वैः कामैः सर्वैर्भोगैः ।

[2] घृतेन ह वा एष देवांस्तर्पयति । य एवं विद्वान् सामान्यहरहः . . . . ।

[3] अमृतेन ह वा . . . . यजूंष्यहरहः . . . . ।

[4] वाकोवाक्यं इतिहासपुराणम् ।

[5] गाथा ।

[6] कुंव्या ।

[7] यथा ह वा एता देवता नेयुर्न कुर्युरेवं हैव तदहर्ब्राह्मणो भवति यदहः स्वाध्यायं नाधीते । तस्मात् स्वाध्यायोऽध्येतव्यस्तस्मादप्यृचं वा यजुर्वा साम वा गाथां वा कुंव्यां वाभिव्याहरेद्व्रतस्याव्यवच्छेदाय ।

I have given these long citations to show the unity and continuity of the tradition of *Upanayana*; from such unity and continuity we are justified in assuming that what is indicated in the *Rigveda* by the passage in the hymn to the frogs is just what is mentioned in the *Taittirīyāraṇyaka* and in the *S'atapatha-Brāhmaṇa* and what is described in the *Gṛhya-Sūtras*. But the *Brahmacārin* mentioned in the *Rigveda* and in the *Atharvaveda* is not the student after *Upanayana*. The word in such contexts has a meaning different from the meaning assigned to the word in the *Brāhmaṇas* and in the *Gṛhya-Sūtras* and other texts on *Dharma-S'āstra*. In the *Rigveda* and in the *Atharvaveda*, *Brahmacarya* means the inquiry into the nature of Brahman and devotion to the realisation of Brahman dealt with in the *Vedas*, while in the later literature it means the pursuit of the study of the texts of the *Vedas*.

There is nothing in the *Rigveda* to show that the students had their studies in the forests. The *Rigvedic* poets were the prominent citizens of the times, who lived in their homes with their family and attended to their civic functions. Although it is not so definitely said there, the *Brahmacārin* of the *Atharvaveda* corresponds to the *Vānaprasthas* (hermits in the forests) of the later period. But in the *Brāhmaṇas* we find that the study has been shifted to the forests, at least the study of the higher stages. In the *Taittirīyāraṇyaka*, the study of the *Veda* in the village is allowed only as a necessity when such study in the forest is found impossible for a student.

This shows that there must have been some cataclysm in the *Vedic* civilization, and the tradition must have been continued by a few families who lived in the forests in retirement during this cataclysm. Perhaps it is after such a cataclysm that the study of the *Vedas* in detail became confined to a single caste, the Brahmins, and the differences in the details relating to vedic study on the basis of caste became so pronounced. Except for such a narrowing down of the field of *Vedic* study, there was no break at all in the *Vedic* tradition ; the same *Upanayana* ceremonial, the same study of what is prescribed for one's own study (*Svādhyāyādhyayana*), continued from the earliest *Vedic* times to the present day through the *Brāhmaṇa* and the *Dharma-S'āstra* periods.

VI. Learning the Meaning

From the passage in the hymn to the frogs in the *Rigveda*, it is found that the study of the recitation of the *Vedic* texts from a teacher must have been the most important aspect of the study of what is prescribed for one's own study. The correct accent, the correct intonation, the correct cadence, all these can be learned only direct from a teacher ; it cannot be accomplished from books, just as singing cannot be learned from books. The question whether the study was meant only for the acquisition of the ability to recite the vedic texts correctly, or whether such study implied the understanding of the meaning also, must have been as old as the *Vedic* period. This is one of the most important points discussed in the later texts on *Mīmāṁsā*. There are two questions involved here. One is whether the *Vedic* texts have a meaning at all; the other is whether the prescribed study contemplated the study of the meaning of the text also, whether it is necessary to study the meaning also to fulfil the prescription of the study (*Svādhāyādhyayana*), whether the understanding of such meaning is only an accidental product of the study of the recitation of the text through the acquaintance of the student in the language.

As a matter of fact, the former is involved in the latter. No sane person can doubt whether there is a meaning at all for such plain text as the *Vedas*. During the discussion, it is only incidentally that the point is raised whether in the *Vedic* texts there are not passages that have no meaning at all or that express contradictory things or that express absurd meanings. The position is this. If a single passage in the *Veda* could be shown to have no meaning at all or to express contradictory or absurd meaning, then it can be established that the study prescribed cannot have the understanding of the meaning as an integral factor; the study is of the whole *Vedic* text and if one sentence has no meaning, the study of the entire text cannot have the understanding of the meaning also as true purport, in so far as this text prescribed has meaningless passages and passages with a contradictory and absurd meaning involved in it.

The question is raised in the first chapter of the *Nirukta* by Yāska as follows:

If it (the *Nirukta*) is for the explanation of the meaning, then they (the texts) are meaningless; so says Kutsa.[1] (I. 15)

This objection consists of the following points:

They have their words associated in a fixed way; and their order also fixed; further there are enjoined (rites) whose forms are accomplished by the *Brāhmaṇas*; further there are (words) that have absurd meanings; further, there are (statements) that are contradictory; further there is instruction to one who (already) knows (it); further it has been said, "Aditi is all"; further there are (words) whose meanings are not clear.[2] (I. 15)

This is the earliest specimen of the problem whether the study of the *Veda* as prescribed implies the study of the meaning also.

On this question there are different views. One view is that the study of the *Vedas* as contained in the prescription, (one shall study what has been prescribed for one's own study) consists of only the study of the words of the *Vedas* to enable the student to recite the texts correctly. The study of the meaning arises as a result of eulogies like:

He is just a pillar that supports a burden[3]

[1] यदि मन्त्रार्थप्रत्ययनायानर्थकं भवतीति कुत्सः।

[2] नियतवाचोयुक्तयो नियतानुपूर्व्या भवन्ति । अथापि ब्राह्मणेन रूपसंपन्ना विधीयन्ते। अथाप्यनुपपन्नार्था भवन्ति। अथापि विप्रतिषिद्धार्था भवन्ति। अथापि जानन्तं संप्रेष्यते। अथाप्याहादितिः सर्वमिति। अथाप्यविस्पष्टार्था भवन्ति।

[3] स्थाणुरयं भारवाहः किलाभूत्।

etc. Another view is that although the prescription enjoins only the study of the recitation of the text, yet when the text is thus studied, the student understands the general meaning of the text also, in so far as the text is in a language which the student understands well through his extra studies; then a desire arises in his mind to have a systematic study of the meaning of the texts. A third position is that the study of the meaning of the text is an integral part of the prescription of the study. The study of the bare text has no purpose and every prescription contains an element of the purpose or the fruit. It is only the text studied according to prescription, with the meaning also understood, that can be utilised in the sacrifices. Thus Skandasvāmin says in the beginning of his commentary on the *Rigveda*:

> In so far as the meaning of the text has to be understood to make the text a fit part (of the sacrifice), this commentary is being written (to enable a student) to understand the meaning of the *Rigveda*.[1]

This is repeated by his disciple Mādhava, in his commentary on the *Sāmaveda*[2] also.

Whatever be the actual scope of the prescription, one thing is certain, and that is that there is emphasis

[1] मन्त्राणामवबोद्धव्यो यतोऽर्थोऽङ्गत्वसिद्धये ।
ऋग्वेदस्यावबोधार्थमतो भाष्यं विरच्यते ॥

[2] एते सर्वे प्रयोगकाले स्वार्थं प्रतिपादयन्तः कर्मणोऽङ्गत्वं प्रतिपद्यन्ते नोच्चारणमात्रेण । . . . . तस्मात्तेऽपि स्वार्थप्रत्यायनेनैव कर्मणोऽङ्गत्वं प्रतिपद्यन्ते । . . . . . एवं सर्वस्तोभानां बोद्धव्योऽर्थो यस्मात् तस्मात् साम्नां केषांचिद्भाष्यं प्रस्तूयते (Sāmaveda, Adyar Library series No. 26.)

on the correct recitation of the vedic texts, while there is also the understanding of the meaning of the texts. Thus any remark that the *Vedas* were studied only for the correct recitation of the texts in a very mechanical way, has no basis in tradition. An intelligent study of the text was actually pursued, whether it was as a part of the prescription or through outside indications or through a personal desire.

VII. Education Universal and Obligatory

The study of the *Veda* along with the accessories (*Vedāṅgas*) is obligatory. It is common to the three castes. I do not want to enter into the question why the citizens outside the three castes were not included in this prescription of an obligatory study. One may as well ask why in the Temple entry Act of Madras, the right to enter the temples was conferred only on the members of a particular religion. The prescription was only for those who accepted the *Vedic* tradition, and those who accepted the *Vedic* tradition consisted of the three castes. This is a minor point. What is really important is the fact that the prescription of the study was obligatory, *i.e.*, the study prescribed was universal. It is difficult to answer the question whether it was also compulsory, besides its being universal. It is not definite what is meant by compulsion. *Mīmāṁsā* does not accept a factor called compulsion in the observance of a prescription. It is faith in the prescription as something that will bring about beneficial fruits that prompts a person to observe the prescription. If there was no *Upanayana* and the subsequent study according to the prescription, then there were social disabilities attached to such non-observance of the prescription ; if this is what is meant by compulsion, then it was a system of universal and *compulsory* study for the citizens. If it meant that there was a temporal power to apply some sanction and that there was a loss or a dimunition of civic rights, then there was no compulsion. *Dharma* flourished in the country through the operation of a sense of *Dharma* and not through the application of a temporal power like the king. As for *Mīmāṁsā*, even a God does not come in as a power to enforce the prescriptions in the *Vedas* ; following God's prescriptions and defending God's ways to man have no position in the *Mīmāṁsā* scheme of *Dharma*. *Mīmāṁsā* depended on the development of character through proper education.

I do not know of any other civilization in this world, where there was such a scheme of universal and obligatory education prescribed to citizens. As a matter of fact, it is this that the prescription amounts to. If there is no *Upanayana* and the subsequent study according to the prescription, a member of the three castes loses his social status. In the case of those who fail in this obligatory duty of education at the prescribed age, it is definitely said :

> One shall have no social intercourse with them.[1]
>
> (Āsv. Gṛhya-Sūtra I-19-7)

[1] नैभिर्व्यवहरेयुः ।

No member of the three castes shall have any dealings with such defaulters.

When there is this prescription relating to the members of the three castes, was there a denial of education to the others? What is enjoined for the members of the three castes is only the sacrament of *Upanayana* and the subsequent study according to a particular method following a specific prescription. Education is free for all. No one was denied education under this prescription. Denial of literacy to some is a factor in a later age, when the civilization had met with a decadence. Even *Mīmāṁsā* prescribes some Vedic study also to persons outside the three castes, like the chieftain of hunters and the carpenters[1] for whom some vedic rites are enjoined. What education was needed for them for citizenship was imparted to them. What the members of the three castes specially received was what they considered obligatory for social status among themselves. When even some sort of Vedic study was permitted for the members outside the three castes, it goes without saying that secular education was freely imparted to them.

Now I take up again the point of the prescription of study as obligatory. There are two schools of *Mīmāṁsakas*. One school follows Prabhākara and the other school follows Kumārila Bhaṭṭa. The two schools are named after these two teachers in *Mīmāṁsā* namely, the *Prābhākara* school and the *Bhāṭṭa* school. Among them there is a difference of view regarding

[1] निषादस्थपति and रथकार ।

the actual prescription that establishes the obligatory nature of the study. The school of Kumārila holds that the passage from the *Taittirīyāraṇyaka*, "one shall study what has been prescribed for one's own study" is the basis for recognising the study as obligatory. But Prabhākara finds some difficulty in accepting this position. The prescription has reference to a boy who cannot be expected to know the meaning of this prescription. And there cannot be a prescription in relation to any one, of anything which that one cannot understand. Therefore he presumes a prescription in the form .

> One shall perform the *Upanayana* of a Brahmin who is eight years old; one shall impart instruction to him.[1]

based on statements like:

> The twice-born, after performing the *Upanayana* of a disciple imparts instruction to him in *Veda* along with the *Kalpas*[2] and the secret meaning[3] they call a Teacher[4] (Manu I, 140).

There is no available text in the *Veda* like this prescription. The study prescribed in the *Taittirīyāraṇyaka* is only a subsidiary to this, which should be accepted as the main prescription. The question may arise

[1] अष्टवर्षं ब्राह्मणमुपनयीत । तमध्यापयीत ।

[2] The laws relating to sacrifices, sacraments and customs.

[3] रहस्य ।

[4] उपनीय तु यः शिष्यं वेदमध्यापयेद्द्विजः ।
सकल्पं सरहस्यं च तमाचार्यं प्रचक्षते ॥

what the fruit is which the teacher gets as a result of acting up this prescription. The answer is that it is the Title of being a Teacher. As a matter of fact, it is this fruit which was most coveted in those days.

The position of the *Bhāṭṭa* School is that even if the boy to be initiated is the person with reference to whom the prescription is to be made, and even if the boy does not at that stage understand the significance of this prescription, his parents know what it is and they can give him proper guidance in acting up to such a prescription. The boy takes to his studies on the advice of the parents who know the meaning of the prescription. There are many other prescriptions which the boy starts observing at that stage without knowing the significance, like the daily ablutions in the morning, noon and evening.[1]

We are not directly concerned with the explanation of the prescription in a literal sense. But there is a very important point raised in this controversy. At least such a point is implied in this. The point is whether it is the obligation of the boy to get educated or whether it is the obligation of the elders to impart education to the boys. To be a teacher is a very covetable position in those days, and to have that Title was a reward in itself for engaging oneself in the profession of teaching. It is not for the sake of any pecuniary profit that people engaged themselves in the profession of teaching. There is the duty of the society to see that all boys are educated,

[1] सन्ध्यावन्दन ।

and those who are learned must offer themselves to discharge such a duty. Of course a teacher was never left in want in those days.

Here there is another point that arises. It is the duty of the teacher to offer and to impart instruction to a boy. Then there is the rule that knowledge shall not be imparted to any one who does not seek it. How can we say that it is the duty of the teacher to offer and to impart instruction. Is it not the duty of the boy to seek such instruction and shall not a teacher impart instruction only to such a seeker of knowledge? There is the following verse:

> Oh! Bharata, every kind of wealth may be given without being asked for. But food, learning and a girl should not be given to those who do not ask for them[1]

Therefore unless there is *Upanayana* of the boy by the parent, one who takes up the profession of teaching cannot impart instruction. Therefore to that extent, the obligatory nature of the study of what has prescribed for one's own study, rests on the statement in the *Taittirīyāraṇyaka.* The boy goes to the teacher as prompted by the parent. When such a boy comes for instruction, then it is the duty of the teacher to accept the pupil and to educate him. To this, the possible reply is that the restriction of imparting instruction to a seeker alone has reference to higher

[1] अयाचितानि देयानि सर्वद्रव्याणि भारत ।
अन्नं विद्या तथा कन्या अनर्थिभ्यो न दीयते ॥

education and not to this obligatory education. Whatever be the basic prescription, there is no doubt about the fact that education of a high standard was an obligatory equipment for full privileges in society, and any one who fails in acquiring this equipment ceases to have the social status.

VIII. Subjects Studied

Now after stating that the education of a certain high standard was an obligatory equipment for all, we will take up the question what the scope of this obligatory education was. It is not what we now call the three R's. Nor is it the mere study of the text of the *Veda* to be able to recite it properly in a mechanical way, without any intellectual side to that study. It has already been said that the learning of the meaning of the *Vedas* is an integral part of the prescription of study. It is not merely the *Vedic* texts that were included in the study, consisting of the texts and the accessories of the *Vedas*; in the *S'atapatha-Brāhmaṇa*, it has been found that the student had to learn, besides the texts of the *Rigveda*, the *Yajurveda* and the *Sāmaveda*, subjects like *Vākovākya*, *Itihāsa* and *Purāṇa*. The passage is:

> And for him who knowing this studies day by day the dialogue, then mythologies and ancient legends as what has been prescribed for his own study (the gods) etc., are pleased.[1]

(S'at-Path. Brāhmaṇa XI-5-7-9)

[1] य एवं विद्वान् वाकोवाक्यमितिहासपुराणमित्यहरहः स्वाध्यायमधीते त एनं तृप्ताः ।

coming after the prescription of the study of the *Rigveda*, the *Yajurveda* and the *Sāmaveda*. The subjects had already been mention in the same text, in the section just preceding this, as :

> He who, knowing this, studies the precepts, the sciences, the dialogues, the mythologies, the ancient legends, songs etc.[1] (S'at-Path-Brahmana XI-5-6-8)

These subjects are included as integral factors in the prescription of study.

In the *Chāndogyopaniṣad*, there is the very interesting story of Nārada approaching Sanatkumāra seeking transcendental wisdom, which he could not learn through his prior studies. Sanatkumāra asks him what it is that he had already studied and what it is that he knew. At this Nārada enumerates the subjects which he had studied as follows :

> I know, oh lord, the *Rigveda*, the *Yajurveda*, the *Sāmaveda*, and the *Atharvaveda* the fourth, the mythologies and the ancient legends which form the fifth book among the *Vedas*, the sciences of the dead ancestors, the sciences of the position of planets etc. (part of astronomy), the science of divination (astrology), the science of hidden treasures, dialogues, the supplemental treatises, the sciences relating to the gods, the sciences relating to Brahman, the sciences relating to the ghosts etc., the science of politics, the science about the stars (a part of astronomy),

[1] य एवं विद्वाननुशासनानि विद्या वाकोवाक्यमितिहासपुराणं गाथा . . . ।

sciences relating to serpents and demi-gods; these, oh lord, I have learned.[1] (*Chāndogyopaniṣad* VII-1-1)

Manu mentions fourteen subjects of study as:

> The four *Vedas* and the (six) accessories thereto, *Mīmāṁsā* (exegesis) logic, ancient legends, moral science: these are the fourteen subjects of study.[2]

It has also been prescribed that the *Vedas* should be studied along with the accessories. These accessories are:

> phonetics, *Kalpa*, grammar, metrics, astronomy, and etymology.[3]

In all places where there is the mention of the study, it is understood that the study consists of all subjects, *Vedas* and also what may be called the secular subjects, besides the *Vedic* accessories (*vedāṅgas*). Thus in the *Raghuvaṁśa* when Kautsa the disciple of Varatantu approached Raghu for gift to enable him to pay his fee to the teacher, Raghu asked what the amount he wanted was, and the reply was:

> I was ordered by the teacher who became irritated at my insisting (the payment of a fee), without

[1] ऋग्वेदं भगवोऽध्येमि यजुर्वेदं सामवेदमाथर्वणं चतुर्थमितिहासपुराणं पञ्चमं वेदानां वेदं पित्र्यं राशिं दैवं निधिं वाकोवाक्यमेकायतनं देवविद्यां ब्रह्मविद्यां भूतविद्यां क्षत्रविद्यां नक्षत्रविद्यां सर्पदेवजनविद्यामेतद्भगवोऽध्येमि ।

[2] अङ्गानि वेदाश्चत्वारो मीमांसा न्यायविस्तरः ।
पुराणं धर्मशास्त्रं च विद्या ह्येताश्चतुर्दश ॥

This is attrributed to Manu, but not found in the text.

[3] शिक्षा कल्पः व्याकरणं छन्दः ज्योतिषं निरुक्तम् ।

considering the smallness of my financial resources, " Bring me fourteen crores (of wealth), calculated on the basis of the fourteen subjects.[1]

(*Raghuvaṁśa* V-21)

Concluding Remarks

If we look into the description of the hermitages of ***Maharishis*** where students were taught, it would be found that there was no subject conceivable that was not included in the course of study. Whether in all such cases the study was the obligatory one prescribed by the passage in the *Taittirīyāraṇyaka* or whether it was only the general study of a later stage, one cannot definitely say. But what is enumerated by Nārada must have been the list of subjects taught as a matter of normal routine. It is after the study of all such subjects that Nārada approached Sanatkumāra for higher wisdom. What has been found in Manu and what has been stated in the *Raghuvaṁśa* and what is associated with the fourteen subjects, must have been included in the normal course of study prescribed for every student, and the study was obligatory. Now we can know what sort of obligatory study was prescribed as a universal equipment in ancient India.

From Aristotle's politics, we find that even in Athens there was a very liberal system of education obtained among the citizens. But there is no mention

1 निर्बन्धसंजातरुषार्थकार्श्यमचिन्तयित्वा गुरुणाहमुक्तः ।
वित्तस्य विद्यापरिसंख्यया मे कोटीश्चतस्रो दश चाहरेति ॥

of such education being obligatory for full social status in Athens. It is true that in the Roman Empire also there was a very high standard of education attained by the students, and such an education was very widely distributed among the citizens also. What is peculiar to the civic life in ancient India is that such education of a high standard was obligatory, and a citizen loses his social status by failing in this obligatory education.

In Europe what liberal education was prescribed for the citizens dwindled in course of time. The traditions of Greece continued in Rome. The Roman Emperors, like the rulers of Greece, were all educated to a very high standard. Some of them were famous writers and philosophers; they were all great patrons of learning also. Alexander was a disciple of Aristotle; Julius Caesar was a great historian and writer; Augustus Caesar who succeeded him was such a great patron of learning that we call a period of literary development in any country as the Augustan period in the history of that country; Marcus Aurelius was the greatest scholar and a famous thinker and writer of his day, and there was no subject known in his time which he did not master. I am only mentioning a few instances for the sake of illustrating my point. Cicero's prose was the standard adopted for the grammar of Latin at a later time. There were also great dramatists and poets in Greece and in Rome whose names have come down to us along with their works. The Roman citizens went to the University of Athens for higher education, and the education of no Roman citizen was considered complete until he had a training in the University of Athens, just as in modern times the education of an Indian youth is not considered complete until he had a training in a Western University also.

But with the fall of the Roman Empire, this tradition of high education for the people also decayed. There followed what is called the Dark Age in Europe. Education was confined to those who were associated with the Church. We know of kings who could neither read nor write and who put their signature in documents with marks like that of an arrow. There was a revival of liberal education in the West only in very recent times, say during the last five hundred years. And even now, education as a necessary factor for full citizenship has not been recognised in the Western countries. Universal primary education is the ultimate goal which they aim at, and which itself has not been attained in many of the countries. Even in such countries where there is compulsory primary education, it has become quite a nominal one; the standard is very low (usually designated by the three R's), and what they study they forget. In their civic life the early education which they received may at best help them just to mark their voting papers, or probably to read some frivolus stuff in cheap journals and other publications.

It is in the light of the present position in the advanced countries of the modern age that we have to consider the condition of education in ancient India.

As I had said already, education was only obligatory; it was not compulsory. In compulsion there is the need for some one with a sanction to enforce the universal education. And such education was universal in India, without any such power to enforce it. The sense of civic duty was the only power that prompted the people to abide by this obligatory universal education, without any sort of compulsion. The tradition was continuous and it was effective also.

I have dealt with the content of the universal and obligatory education; in the next lecture I will take up the purpose of this very high standard of education kept in view in ancient India. In a word I may say here that the primary purpose was to develop a very healthy civic life in the country.

LECTURE II

I. True Purpose of Education

AMONG the various systems of philosophy and religion in latter-day India there are two systems, the *Pūrva* (prior) and the *Uttara* (latter) *Mīmāṁsās*, which have their *Sūtra* literature starting with:

> Then therefore, the desire to know *Dharma* [1]

and

> Then therefore, the desire to know Brahman,[2]

respectively. In both the systems the *Sūtras* have been accepted as based on the prescription:

> One should study what has been prescribed for one's own study.[3]

The word "then" has been interpreted as meaning "after the study of what has been prescribed for one's own study". Thus S'abarasvāmin says in his *Bhāṣya* on the *Mīmāṁsā Sūtras*:

> Here, in ordinary usage, the word "then" has been seen as doing something that follows what has

[1] अथातो धर्मजिज्ञासा ।

[2] अथातो ब्रह्मजिज्ञासा ।

[3] स्वाध्यायोऽध्येतव्यः ।

taken place; here nothing has been obtained (like that). There must be such a thing, which having existed, the desire to know *Dharma* is settled as following. . . . But that is the study of the *Vedas*. . . The Teacher[1] has used the word "then" in respect of such a desire to know *Dharma*, which is impossible without the study of the *Vedas*. . . . Having surely first of all accomplished the study of the *Vedas*, thereafter there should be the desire to know *Dharma*.[2] (I-1-1)

Here it is asserted that the study of the meaning of the *Vedas* is an integral part of the implication of the prescription, "One should study what has been prescribed for one's own study."

There are other Schools of thought regarding the position of the "consideration of the meaning" in relation to the prescription. In the *Uttara Mīmāṁsā*, usually known as *Vedānta*, there are different views on the subject. There is the School of thought that the prescription, "One should study what has been prescribed for one's own study" is in itself confined to the study of the recitation of the *Vedas* and that the study of the meaning of the *Vedas* comes in only

[1] Jaimini, the author of the *Sūtras*.

[2] तत्र लोके अयमथशब्दः वृत्तादनन्तरस्य प्रक्रियार्थो दृष्टः । नेह किंचिदुपलभ्यते । भवितव्यं तु तेन यस्मिन् सति अनन्तरं धर्मजिज्ञासा अवकल्प्यते । . . . . तत्तु वेदाध्ययनम् । . . . तादृशीं तु धर्मजिज्ञासामधिकृत्य अथशब्दं प्रयुक्तवानाचार्यः या वेदाध्ययनमन्तरेण न संभवति । . . . . . . वेदाध्ययनमेव पूर्वमभिनिर्वर्त्य अनन्तरं धर्मो जिज्ञासितव्यः ।

through "Eulogistic"[1] passages glorifying the knowledge of the meaning of the *Vedas* and also condemning ignorance of such meaning. There is another School according to which the word "then" in "Then therefore, the desire to know Brahman" means "After the consideration of *Dharma* in the *Pūrva Mīmāṁsā*." S'aṅkarācārya says that the term "then" denotes "the attainment of the four-fold means":

> Discrimination of things eternal and transient, detachment from fruits (of actions) here and hereafter, acquisition of calmness and discipline, and desire for release.[2] (S'ūtrabhāṣya I-1-1)

But he too definitely says that "the study of what has been prescribed for one's own study" is necessary:

> But the study of what has been prescribed for one's own study is common.[3] (Sūtrabhāṣya I-1-1)

It is a common factor whether the meaning of the words "then" is "after the knowledge of *Dharma*" or whether it is "after the attainment of the four-fold means".

Thus the purpose and consequence of the prescription, "One should study what has been prescribed for one's own study" is to consider the problems of *Dharma* and *Brahman*. In *Mīmāṁsā*,[4] *Dharma* does not mean any kind of civic duty. It is taken in a

[1] अर्थवाद ।

[2] नित्यानित्यवस्तुविवेक: इहामुत्रफलभोगविराग: शमदमादिसंपत् मुमुक्षुत्वं च ।

[3] स्वाध्यायाध्ययनं तु समानम् ।

[4] That is the Pūrva Mīmāṁsā itself.

Heaven. When in a drama there is the benediction like:

> May that S'iva (Sthāṇu) easily attainable through steady devotion, be for your happiness.[1]
>
> (Vikramorvas'īya)

> May that S'iva destroy your dark mental activities to enable you to see the right Path.[2] (Mālavikāgnimitra)

and

> May S'iva (Īs'a), endowed with these tangible eight-fold body, protect you.[3] (S'ākuntala)

what is it that is prayed for? It cannot be certainly the procurement of Divine Grace as a step for the attainment of Heaven, or such religious merit. It must be the protection against evil forces that prevent a person from appreciating the beauty of the drama that is presented on the stage. Similarly, the study of grammar brings about some transcendental fruit in the person which cannot be explained through any visible fruit.

Now let us take metre (*Chandas*) which goes along with the proper recitation of the *Vedas*. In these days we do not *recite* poetry, we do not even read poetry; we simply *look* into poetry as represented by a few scripts in a written or printed book. In doing this, we are losing a good part of poetry and its true beauty; I may even say that we completely miss the beauty by

[1] स स्थाणुः स्थिरभक्तियोगसुलभो निःश्रेयसायास्तु वः ।

[2] सन्मार्गालोकनाय व्यपनयतु स वस्तामसीं वृत्तिमीशः ।

[3] प्रत्यक्षाभिः प्रपन्नस्तनुभिरवतु वस्ताभिरष्टाभिरीशः ।

and knowledge come primarily within the scope of the prescription, "One should study what has been prescribed for one's own study." Now the question must be considered whether the performance of the *Yāgas* and the contemplation of the nature of *Brahman* form the sole purpose of the study of the *Vedas*. One cannot deny these as purposes. But what I consider is whether there are other purposes too.

In the *Taittirīyopaniṣad* there is the famous passage which contains the instruction that the teacher imparts to the disciple at the end of his study [1], when he is to leave the teacher for his home to enter the stage of a house-holder. Since the passage is well known to nearly all, it is not necessary to cite the entire passage here. But it will be necessary to cite and interpret select pieces from this famous passage. The passage starts as follows:

> After teaching the *Vedas*, the teacher instructs the disciple: speak Truth, observe *Dharma*.[2]

It has always been a wonder to me why the two statements are given in this order. "Speak truth" can have reference to the knowledge of the Absolute, the ultimate Reality. "Observe *Dharma*" can have reference to the knowledge and performance of *Dharma* in the form of *Yāgas*. If this is so, why is it that the two statements occur in this order? In so far as the two *Mīmāṁsās* begin respectively as, "Then therefore,

[1] Tait. Up. I. 11.

[2] वेदमनूच्याचार्योऽन्तेवासिनमनुशास्ति । सत्यं वद । धर्मं चर ।

the desire to know *Dharma*" and "Then therefore, the desire to know *Brahman*," we should expect the order as "Observe *Dharma*" and "Speak truth". First one should perform all the prescribed *Yagas* forming *Dharma*, and then one must realise Truth.

From the *Vedānta* point of view, there is a possible explanation that the final purport, "Speak truth" is given first, being the most important and the other, being subsidiary, is given later. But in the case of the *Mīmāṁsā*, which recognises "knowledge" (*Jñāna*) as a factor in higher life only in a very halting way, such an explanation is impossible. May be that we can also say that the understanding of the nature of the *Yāgas*, consisting of the various elements of the *Yāgas* like the performer and the Deity, is first prescribed, and then the performance of the *Yāgas* is given, in the natural order.

I would have easily entertained either of these two explanations if the subsequent pieces in the passage in this section conformed to such an interpretation. What is the next passage? It is as follows:

> After offering to the teacher money that will please him, thou shall not break the continuance of your (family) line.[1]

According to *Mīmāṁsā*, there follows *Snāna* (Ceremonial Bath marking the termination of study) and marriage. Then, when a son is born and when the

[1] आचार्याय प्रियं धनमाहृत्य प्रजातन्तुं मा व्यवच्छेत्सीः ।

householder is not yet aged, he performs the ceremony of kindling the sacred fire. It is said:

> He for whom a son has been born and who has black hair, shall kindle the sacred fire.[1]

This passage may be construed as referring to this prescription. The next passage is:

> One shall not show neglect in the matter of worship to gods and to dead ancestors.[2]

and this supports the previous view. But it is very difficult to give a satisfactory interpretation from the *Vedānta* point of view. I realise that the *Vedāntins*, even the *Advaitins* (monists) are not averse to marriage and to the rites prescribed for performance after marriage. My point is that there is no emphasis on the acquisition of *Brahman*-knowledge in this passage, which one should expect if the first sentence in the section had reference to the *Sūtra*: "Then, therefore, the desire to know *Brahman*" of the *Vedānta* system.

Even from the *Mīmāṁsā* point of view, let us see if there is any special emphasis on the *Yāgas*. Before the sentence: "One shall not show neglect in the matter of worship to gods and to dead ancestors," there are many instructions regarding factors in life in which the student shall show no neglect, like:

> one shall not show neglect in the matter of truth;
> one shall not show neglect in the matter of *Dharma*;
> one shall not show neglect in the matter of welfare;

[1] जातपुत्रः कृष्णकेशः अग्नीनादधीत ।

[2] देवपितृकार्याभ्यां न प्रमदितव्यम् ।

one shall not show neglect in the matter of prosperity; one shall not show neglect in the matter of the study of what is prescribed for one's own study and of expounding it.[1]

Here we do not find any specific mention of the various *yāgas*. One may wonder why there is not a definite instruction regarding the *Yāgas*. After this there is the instruction to show due respect to the parents, to the teachers, and to guests. There follows the instruction to be of good behaviour, presumably in civic life:

Which actions are not condemned, they must be adopted; not the others. What are our approved conducts, they must be respected by you; not the others.[2]

After a statement about gifts, there is the instruction regarding doubts about the nature of *Dharma* and what is good conduct:

Then, if you may have a desire to discriminate what is *Dharma* or a desire to discriminate what is (good) conduct, those Brahmins that may be there who are thoughtful, who are *Yukta*, who are *Āyukta*[3] and who are attached to *Dharma*, you shall conduct

[1] सत्यान्न प्रमदितव्यम् । धर्मान्न प्रमदितव्यम् । कुशलान्न प्रमदितव्यम् । भूत्यै न प्रमदितव्यम् । स्वाध्यायप्रवचनाभ्यां न प्रमदितव्यम् ।

[2] यान्यनवद्यानि कर्माणि तानि सेवितव्यानि । नो इतराणि । यान्यस्माकं सुचरितानि तानि त्वयोपास्यानि । नो इतराणि ।

[3] These two terms युक्त and आयुक्त are explained as "attached" to good conduct, and "dedicated" by oneself.

yourself in such matters in that way in which they conduct themselves.[1]

There is a similar instruction relation to desire to discriminate who are undesirable persons:

Then, in matter of those who are condemned etc.[2]

If the performance of the *Yāgas* and the realisation *Brahman* are the ends kept in view for the prescription: "One shall study what has been prescribed for one's own study", it is surprising that in such an important context, there is no specific mention of either the performance of the *Yāgas* or about the ultimate realisation of *Brahman*. From the whole trend of the instruction, one is not wrong in concluding that the real purpose of the study of the *Veda* under a teacher is to make a student a worthy citizen, and all items enumerated here are very important in the civic life of the nation. The study of the *Vedas* under the teacher consists of not merely the training in the proper recitation of the text of the *Vedas*, nor in understanding the meaning of such texts; the study is of the *Vedas* along with the auxiliary texts (*Vedāṅgas*), which contain *Dharmaśāstra* (Law-texts) as a part of the *Kalpas*, *Vyākaraṇa* and *Chandas*.

In the case of the study of the *Dharmaśāstra* as part of the study of the *Vedas* under a teacher, there is a great principle in civic life propounded, namely, that

[1] अथ यदि ते धर्मविचिकित्सा वा वृत्तविचिकित्सा वा स्यात् ये तत्र ब्राह्मणाः संमर्शिनः युक्ता आयुक्ता धर्मकामाः स्युः यथा ते तत्र वर्तेरन् तथा तत्र वर्तेथाः ।

[2] अथाभ्याख्यातेषु ।

it is not enough if a citizen conducts himself in his civic life according to the law of the country; for a true, orderly civic life, the citizen must also ***know*** what the law is and then conduct himself according to such law known by him. This is the only safeguard for the permanence of orderly life in a country. In the *Mīmāṁsā*, this problem has been dealt with in its own context. The context in the *Mīmāṁsā* is that of *Yāgas*. And there the question has been raised why one should know the meaning of the text of the *Vedas*, why one should not rest content with the interpretations and directions relating to the texts contained in other works. They cite the example of the passage :

> (Reciting) " spread wide ", one spreads (the sacrifical cake).[1]

Is it not enough if the person who is to do the act gets the direction about what he has to do, indirectly ? Is it necessary that he should have a direct knowledge of the action from the text itself ? The answer given is that he must know what he has to do from the text itself directly and that he should not rest content with indirect knowledge. I will cite the discussion on the problem from the *Jaiminīya-Nyāya-Mālā-Vistara* of Sāyaṇa, where the whole point is considered very briefly and at the same time in a very lucid way also :

> Are *Mantras* (formulas) like " Spread wide " only for producing some unseen fruit, or do they also reveal the action of spreading the cakes etc.?

[1] उरु प्रथस्वेति प्रथयति ।

Since that (action) has been revealed by the *Brāhmaṇa* text also, they are only the cause of a spiritual fruit.

No; because the revealing of that is a seen fruit and because a seen fruit is superior to an unseen fruit.[1]
(I-2-11 and 12)

There is a certain *Mantra* "Spread wide". ... This and other *Mantras*, being recited during the performance of the *Yāgas*, produce simply an unseen fruit. But their recitation is not to manifest a meaning; because the meaning in the form of spreading the cake has been understood even from the passage in the *Brāhmaṇas*.[2]

This is not reasonable. When there is the possibility of there being the seen purpose of manifesting the meaning, it is not possible to assume a mere unseen one. Therefore, the purpose of reciting the *Mantra* in the performance of the *Yāga* is only to remind the meaning, which is a seen (fruit) When there is the possibility of reminding the meaning even from the *Brāhmaṇa* passage, for the regulation that it

[1] मन्त्रा उरु प्रथस्वेति किमदृष्टैकहेतव: ।
यागेषूत पुरोडाशप्रथनादेश्च भासका: ॥
ब्राह्मणेनापि तद्भानान्मन्त्रा: पुण्यैकहेतव: ।
न ; तद्भानस्य दृष्टत्वाद्दृष्टं वरमदृष्टत: ॥

[2] उरु प्रथस्वेत्ययं कश्चिन्मन्त्र: । . . . . . एवमादयो मन्त्रा यागप्रयोगेषूच्चार्यमाणा अदृष्टमेव जनयन्ति । न तु अर्थप्रकाशनाय तदुच्चारणम् । पुरोडाशप्रथनलक्षणस्यार्थस्य ब्राह्मणवाक्येनापि प्राप्तत्वात् ।

> should be reminded only by the *Mantras*, let there be an unseen fruit, in so far as there cannot be a seen fruit for that.[1]

This is the presentation of the problem in a brief way. If we transfer this ritualistic interpretation to the context that will suit civic life, it comes to this that it is not enough if a citizen leaves matters of law to his lawyer or to second-hand sources of information of other kinds. Every citizen must know law for himself and must conduct himself according to the provisions of law as a result of his direct knowledge of law. Thus the study of law as an integral part of the general study which is obligatory to every citizen under the prescription: "One shall study what has been prescribed for one's own study," which is common to the three castes, has a definite purpose and a real purpose. But to the question why he should know law for himself, from original sources, first hand and directly, why it is not enough if he conducts himself according to the provision of law as a result of second-hand and indirect knowledge from other texts or from advisers, the only reply is that it is not possible to state a "concrete purpose."[2] It is necessary for the continuity of life according to law in a country. The purpose of

[1] नैतद्युक्तम् । अर्थप्रत्यायनस्य दृष्टप्रयोजनस्य संभवे सति केवलादृष्टस्य कल्पयितुमशक्यत्वात । तस्माद्दृश्यमानार्थानुस्मरणमेव यागप्रयोगे मन्त्रोच्चारणस्य प्रयोजनम् । ब्राह्मणवाक्येनापि अर्थानुस्मरणसंभवे मन्त्रेणैवानुस्मरणीयमिति यो नियमः तस्य दृष्टासंभवात् अदृष्टं प्रयोजनमस्तु ।

[2] दृष्टप्रयोजन ।

religious rites is the acquisition of such unseen fruits like heaven. It is the postulation of a similar unseen fruit even in civic life which gives the civic life in India a religious colour. Besides the concrete result there is also an unseen fruit realised by observing certain specific standards.

At present, ignorance of law is not an excuse in modern legal procedure. This principle has been accepted not as a consequence of the obligation on the part of every citizen to know law for himself; it is only a legal fiction adopted for convenience in the administration of law. If such a fiction is not adopted, the burden of proof that the party knew law while straying away from the path of law also comes in, and that may delay, and even vitiate, the administration of law. But in ancient India, ignorance of law, and that from the original sources and directly, could not be brought in as an excuse for deviation from the path of law, in so far as it was obligatory for every citizen to know law. Thus what is now only a legal fiction adopted for conveniences in the proper administration of law, was recognised as a fundamental in the civic life of the nation in ancient India. In this way, in ancient India law prevailed because everyone knew law and everyone conducted himself according to the provision of law, not because there was a power above to enforce law. Such cases for the need to enforce law from outside were, consequently, reduced to a minimum; such cases could not, certainly, be eliminated totally.

Of the six *Vedāṅgas* (auxiliary texts for the study of the *Vedas*) I selected three, namely, ***Dharma*** (Law), *Vyākaraṇa* (Grammar) and ***Chandas*** (Prosody) with a specific purpose. *Vyākaraṇa* was necessary, because it was not enough if educated people knew the language as a practical instrument for communication of ideas. It is also necessary that one should speak correct language. and elegant language also. Patañjali discusses this problem in his *Mahābhāṣya* in his own masterly way:

> He who uses words following the science (of grammar), is associated with eminence. . . . Or then, let it be that there is *Dharma* in the knowledge (of correct language). Now, it has been said that if there is *Dharma* in knowledge, there is *Adharma* (evil) too in the same way. This is not a defect. We take what has been explicitly said as authority. . . . And what is explicitly said says that there is *Dharma* in the knowledge of (correct) words, but not that there is *Adharma* (evil) in the knowledge of wrong words. Or, the knowledge of wrong words is certainly a means of knowing correct words. He who knows what are wrong words knows also what are correct words. In this way, to him who says that there is *Dharma* in knowledge (of correct words) it comes about by implication that there is *Dharma* in the knowledge of (correct) words preceded by the knowledge of wrong words. Or this can be like one who digs a well. It is thus. Although one who digs a well gets smeared with dust and clay, he, when

water is obtained, secures such a benefit from that (water) itself. . . . Here too, although there may be *Adharma* in the knowledge of wrong words, by such *Dharma* which abides in the knowledge of (correct) words, that evil will be destroyed; there will be association with greater eminence.[1] (Paspaśāhnika).

What is this eminence (*Abhyudaya*)? Of course one can easily say that it is the attainment of heaven through some unseen fruit. But when language was a living one, this eminence could have been only the recognition of speaking correct and elegant language and the consequent eminence in civic life. That is *Dharma* in *Vyākaraṇa*. It is the obligation of every citizen to speak a language that is worthy of an educated man.

Dharma is the means for the attainment of Heaven in religion. But *Dharma* is the means for the attainment of social eminence in civic life, and correct and elegant speech is an aspect of civic life. Whenever we see the word *Dharma*, we should not introduce the pure religion aspect, as a means for the attainment of

[1] शास्त्रपूर्वकं य: शब्दान् प्रयुङ्क्ते सोऽभ्युदयेन युज्यते । . . . . अथवा पुनरस्तु ज्ञान एव धर्म इति । ननु चोक्तं ज्ञाने धर्म इति चेत तथा अधर्म इति । नैष दोष: । शब्द-प्रमाणका वयम् । . . . . शब्दश्च शब्दज्ञाने धर्ममाह नापशब्दज्ञानेऽधर्मम् । . . . . अथवाभ्युपाय एवापशब्दज्ञानं शब्दज्ञाने । योऽपशब्दान् जानाति शब्दानप्यसौ जानाति । तदेवं ज्ञाने धर्म इति ब्रुवत: अर्थादापन्नं भवति अपशब्दज्ञानपूर्वके शब्दज्ञाने धर्म इति । अथवा कूपखानकवदेतद्भविष्यति । तद्यथा । कूपखानक: कूपं खनन् यद्यपि मृदा पांसुभिश्चावकीर्णो भवति सोऽप्सु संजातासु तत एव तं गुणमासादयति । . . . . . इहापि यद्यप्यपशब्दज्ञाने अधर्म: तथापि यस्त्वसौ शब्दज्ञाने धर्म: तेन च स दोषो निर्घानिष्यते । भूयसा चाभ्युदयेन योगो भविष्यति ।

Heaven. When in a drama there is the benediction like:

> May that S'iva (Sthāṇu) easily attainable through steady devotion, be for your happiness.[1]
>
> (Vikramorvas'īya)

> May that S'iva destroy your dark mental activities to enable you to see the right Path.[2] (Mālavikāgnimitra)

and

> May S'iva (Īs'a), endowed with these tangible eight-fold body, protect you.[3] (S'ākuntala)

what is it that is prayed for? It cannot be certainly the procurement of Divine Grace as a step for the attainment of Heaven, or such religious merit. It must be the protection against evil forces that prevent a person from appreciating the beauty of the drama that is presented on the stage. Similarly, the study of grammar brings about some transcendental fruit in the person which cannot be explained through any visible fruit.

Now let us take metre (*Chandas*) which goes along with the proper recitation of the *Vedas*. In these days we do not *recite* poetry, we do not even read poetry; we simply *look* into poetry as represented by a few scripts in a written or printed book. In doing this, we are losing a good part of poetry and its true beauty; I may even say that we completely miss the beauty by

[1] स स्थाणुः स्थिरभक्तियोगसुलभो निःश्रेयसायास्तु वः ।

[2] सन्मार्गालोकनाय व्यपनयतु स वस्तामसीं वृत्तिमीशः ।

[3] प्रत्यक्षाभिः प्रपन्नस्तनुभिरवतु वस्ताभिरष्टाभिरीशः ।

simply *looking* into poetry printed in a book. *Veda* is high class poetry composed by great poets of those times. The authors were only the *medium* for the flow of true poetry; really they were not the *authors*. True poetry is a *fact* in Nature and not a *product* of any one's mental activity. That poetry flows through a proper medium, whom we designate as the poet. That is why the *Vedic* texts were regarded as transcending the person (of the poet), *i. e. Apauruṣeya*, being the true poetry of the time. They must be recited with proper accent and intonation; there shall not be any change in the words; no word shall be substituted by another word; and the words shall not be recited in any other order too. That is the true nature of high class poetry. Apart from command of correct and elegant language, literary eminence too was considered as an obligatory equipment of every true citizen.

What is contemplated in the prescription, "One shall study what has been prescribed as one's own study", is a very liberal, all-round education of a very high standard, calculated to prepare the student for a useful life in the State as a worthy citizen. No one can ignore the fact that there are the *Brāhmaṇa* texts prescribing the various *Yāgas* and the *Upaniṣads* dealing with the problem of the Ultimate Truth. Therefore eligibility and ability to understand the nature of the *Yāgas* and the nature of *Brahman*, and ability to perform the *Yāgas* and other rituals and to contemplate on the Supreme Truth, cannot be ruled out from the purpose of education. What I want to emphasise is the importance of the civic life aspect of education in the *Vedic* times.

In an earlier part of this discourse I had said that although the prescription, " One shall study what has been prescribed for one's own study," appears in a very late part of the *Vedic* literature, namely, towards the middle of the *Taittirīyāraṇyaka*, yet the system found there must be as old as even the earliest part of the *Rigveda*, if not still earlier. At this stage we must take note of the fact that the *Ṛṣis* of the *Rigveda* were different from the *Ṛṣis* of later times, *i. e.*, the *Ṛṣis* of the *Upaniṣads* and the *Purāṇas.* The *Rigvedic Ṛṣis* were the top-ranking citizens of the times, leading their normal civic life as house-holders, who were also great poets with transcendental powers of vision. The *Yāgas* were quite current in those times as national institutions, and they had a clear vision of the Absolute also. There is no evidence at all in the Vedic texts themselves to show that the *Yāgas* of the complicated nature found described in the *Brāhmaṇas* and in the *Sūtra* literature of a later period were subsequent concoctions and manipulations, and that the problem of the Absolute was new to the *Upaniṣads*, of which only hazy notions were found in the *Saṁhitās* (original texts) of the *Vedas*. As a matter of fact, neither the *Brāhmaṇas* nor the *Upaniṣads* developed anything that can be called radically new; they simply discussed the problems already found fully developed in the *Vedic Saṁhitās*.

The real spirit of the *Vedas* is one of harmonious blending of the secular life with religion and philosophy.

It is this spirit that we find in the system of education contemplated in the prescription, "One shall study what has been prescribed for one's own study." All were educated and they were educated to get themselves prepared to be worthy citizens of a civilized State. Literature and arts, religion and philosophy were all integral parts of that civic life.

II. Obligatory and Optional Courses

At this stage I have again to take up the question: at what stage did the student leave the teacher and at what stage was the instruction contained in the *Taittirīyopaniṣad*, given to the student by the teacher? It was found that normally a Brahmin was initiated to study (*Upanayana*) at the age of eight. Then it has been prescribed that he shall stay at the teacher's household as a student for twelve years. The *Snāna* (Ceremonial Bath marking the termination of study) came after that. That is, the student finished his studies at the age of twenty. There are certain prescriptions that he may stay at the teacher's household for periods of twelve years for each of the four *Vedas*, that he may study all the four *Vedas* or study only three, two or one. He must study at least one and that is why the period of twelve years for study has been prescribed as the minimum.

The student understands the general meaning of the *Vedas* at this stage, although the real study seems to be only to enable him to recite the *Vedas* properly. What is contemplated by the *Sūtras*:

> Then therefore, the desire to know *Dharma*

and

> Then therefore, the desire to know *Brahman*

is only the critical study of the *Vedas*, the *Vicāra*. If study in the prescription, "One shall study what has been prescribed for one's own study," is only the training in the recitation of the *Vedas*, then there is the other prescription:

> One shall perform the Ceremonial Bath after his study.[1]

As soon as the study is over, he shall perform the Bath, which marks the termination of the study. Then where does the critical study (*Vicāra*) come in? This point has been taken up by S'abarasvāmin in his *Bhāṣya* on the *Mīmāṁsāsūtras*:

> But when the Veda has been studied, two (courses) are open; one has to return from the teacher's household; and one has to make a critical study of the *Vedic* texts. The purpose of this teaching is this: one shall not return from the teacher's household; how one shall study the texts of the *Vedas* critically. If this be so, then the study of the *Vedas* is not the antecedent of the desire to know *Dharma*. Indeed there is this *Vedic* statement: after studying the *Vedas*, one shall perform the Ceremonial Bath.

[1] अधीत्य स्नायात्.

And here, one who should perform the Ceremonial Bath after studying the *Vedas*, transgresses this *Vedic* passage if he desires to know *Dharma*. And a *Vedic* passage shall not, really, be transgressed. Here it is said: we shall transgress this *Vedic* passage; if we do not transgress it, we shall be declaring the *Vedas*, which have a meaning, as not having a meaning. . . . And the great people who are well-versed in *Yāgas*, do not speak of the fruit merely from the study. . . . And there is not prescribed here the immediate sequence of the Ceremonial Bath for one who has studied the *Vedas*. Indeed here there is no word which express immediate sequence; the (termination) ***ktvā*** (which means "having done") is declared as having the meaning of priority in time, not immediate sequence.[1] (I-1-1)

The difficulty is that the terms of the prescription, "One shall study what has been prescribed for one's own study" are satisfied with the study of the recitation of the *Vedic* texts. After the study prescribed by this statement, there must be the return to the home of the student from the household of the teacher. There

[1] अधीते वेदे द्वयमापतति । गुरुकुलाच्च समावर्तितव्यं वेदवाक्यानि च विचारयितव्यानि । तत्र गुरुकुलान्मा समावर्तिष्ट कथं नु वेदवाक्यानि विचारयेत इत्येवमर्थोऽयमुपदेशः । यद्येवं न तर्हि वेदाध्ययनं पूर्वं धर्मजिज्ञासायाः । एवं हि समामनन्ति—वेदमधीत्य स्नायात्—इति । इह च वेदमधीत्य स्नास्यन् धर्मं जिज्ञासमान इममाम्नायमतिक्रामेत् । न चाम्नायो नामातिक्रमितव्यः । तदुच्यते । अतिक्रमिष्याम इममाम्नायम् । अनतिक्रामन्तो वेदमर्थवन्तं सन्तं अनर्थकं कल्पयेम । . . . . न च तत्र अध्ययनमात्रात् तत्रभवन्तो याज्ञिकाः फलं समामनन्ति । . . . . न चाधीतवेदस्य स्नानानन्तर्यमेतद्विधीयते । न ह्यत्रानन्तर्यस्य वक्ता कश्चिच्छब्दोऽस्ति । पूर्वकालतायां क्त्वा स्मर्यते नानन्तर्यें ।

must also be the critical study of the *Vedic* texts (*Vicāra*), S'abarasvāmin tries to overcome this difficulty by saying that the return from the teacher's household need not be immediately after the termination of the training in the recitation of the *Vedic* texts, but only after a further term of study in a critical way. S'abarasvāmin's difficulty was that since the *Vedas* have a meaning and since it is only the *Vedic* texts studied along with the meaning that can be utilised in the *Yāgas*, termination of study with the mere training in the recitation of the *Vedic* texts will be against this aspect of the study, and later utilisation, of the *Vedas*.

But there is another aspect of the question, which may solve the difficulty. There are two kinds of the study of the meaning of the *Vedas*. One is the study of the meaning of the texts in a general way, which must be easy for a student who knows the language and literature and all such accessories needed for understanding the meaning of the text, like grammar and lexicography. This is the only obligatory study prescribed for the *Vedas*. The later critical study is optional. For this critical study, he may stay on in the household of the teacher and this is only optional. Yet he can perform the Ceremonial Bath, after the obligatory study. He can also return home and then come back for the further study of a critical nature.

The only difficulty in this explanation is that if he performs the Ceremonial Bath and then resumes his stay in the teacher's household for the further critical study, he remains a *Snātaka* (one who has performed the Ceremonial Bath marking the termination of the stage of discipleship, but who has not married and entered the stage of a householder). Such a *Snātaka* does not belong to any of the four stages in life (*Āśramas*). Every *Dvija* (twice-born) must remain in one or other of the four stages in life. After the Ceremonial Bath, marriage has been prescribed.

Here we must consider if marriage was obligatory, in actual practice. If the kindling of the sacred fire is an obligatory rite for every twice-born, then marriage is necessary, since the kindling of the sacred fire can be performed only when a son is born to him. But we know actually that there are many *Snātakas* mentioned in literature. All the Brahmins who accompanied Yudhiṣṭhira to the forest after his defeat in the game of gambling and his forfeiture of his kingdom to Suyodhana, his cousin, were *Snātakas*. Therefore we can say easily that even after the Ceremonial Bath, a student can continue his studies as a *Snātaka*, without finally returning home. But if the Ceremonial Bath implies also the final return of the student to his own home after completing *all* his studies, this explanation is not satisfactory.

Taking into consideration the actual practice obtaining in the country, it is noted that there are communities among whom it is obligatory that the Ceremonial Bath should be performed at a certain age; it is at the age of about sixteen. Some communities perform this Ceremonial Bath even at an earlier age, at fourteen. Then they remain a *Snātaka*, if they do not marry. There are other communities among whom they remain as a *Brahmacārin* without performing the Ceremonial Bath, until their marriage. Although there are prohibitions against a person finishing one stage and not entering the next stage, *i.e.*, remaining a *Snātaka*, found in texts, there is no doubt about the fact that in actual practice there were such *Snātakas*, who do not belong to any of the four stages in life.

There are certain discrepancies. The initiation for study is at the age of eight and the study prescribed is for twelve years; then the Ceremonial Bath must be performed, and this must naturally be at the age of twenty. But there are communities who perform the Ceremonial Bath at the age of sixteen and even earlier. To say that a person should marry after the Ceremonial Bath, if the Bath is at the age of sixteen, is also absurd; this is too early an age for marriage. Then the study is of the recitation of the *Vedas*, and after this the Ceremonial Bath must be performed; and there must also be the study of the meaning of the *Vedas*, for which latter we find no time.

The only way in which I can find some sort of explanation is to assume that there are two stages in the education of a student. There is the obligatory portion of training in the recitation of the *Vedic* texts, along with the various auxiliary texts (*Vedāṅgas*); there is aslo the optional portion of a further critical study of the *Vedas*. The bare study of the meaning of the *Vedas* in a general way comes in as a natural element in the obligatory study, in so far as the student is equipped for such a study by his knowledge of the language and literature and the auxiliary texts like grammar and lexicography. What is required for utilising the texts of the *Vedas* later in the *Yāgas* is only a knowledge of the meaning of the texts of the *Vedas* and not a critical knowledge of the text.

In this way we come to three stages in the career of a student. There is the elementary study at home before the initiation (*Upanayana*); there is the obligatory study after the initiation; lastly there is the optional study of a higher and critical nature after the Ceremonial Bath marking the termination of the obligatory study. Admitting all the limitations in comparison, I may assert that these three stages may be equated with the elementary education, the secondary education and the college education in modern times. The first is a necessary preliminary to the second stage which is prescribed as obligatory for all the youths. The last is optional. The obligatory course lasted for eight years and the optional for four years. Thus the course equated with the modern secondary education finished at the age of sixteen; and the education of an optional nature equated with the college course ended at the age of twenty.

The prescription, " One shall study what has been prescribed for one's own study " comprehends only the obligatory eight years course. Then there is the advanced study contemplated by the *Sūtras*, " Then therefore, the desire to know *Dharma*," and " Then therefore, the desire to know *Brahman*," which lasts for four years. One is not sure whether the instruction found in the *Taittirīyopaniṣad*, which was considered just before, comes at the end of the obligatory course or at the end of the whole education ; those who finish at the end of the obligatory course may receive it then, and those who undergo the further course may receive it at the end of the whole course ; it can as well be that all received the instruction at the end of the obligatory course. As for understanding the meaning of the *Vedic* texts, it is not said that there should be a critical study ; what is obligatory is only to understand the meaning, not a critical study of the texts. As for the *Sūtra*, " Then therefore, the desire to know *Dharma*," what S'abarasvāmin says is that there shall be the critical study and not the understanding the meaning. The word he uses is *Vicāra* (critical investigation) and not *Arthāvabodha* (understanding the meaning). His statement is : " but when the Veda has been studied, two (courses) are open ; one has to return from the teacher's household and one has to make a critical study of the Vedic texts." Certainly there is a difference between knowing the meaning and making a critical study. For knowing the meaning, what is wanted is only Etymology (*Nirukta*). Grammar (*Vyākaraṇa*) etc. It is not necessary to take to *Mīmāṁsā* for this. Thus it has been said in the *Nirukta* :

> Then again, there will be no understanding of the meaning in respect of the *Mantras*.[1] (I-15)

[1] अथापीदमन्तरेण मन्त्रेष्वर्थप्रत्ययो न भवति

It is this understanding of the meaning that is inherent in the prescription, "One shall study what has been prescribed for one's own study" and not the critical study contemplated in the *Mīmāṁsā S'ūtra*, "Then therefore, the desire to know Dharma." Passages like:

> He will become a pillar bearing a burden who after studying the *Vedas* does not know the meaning; he who knows the meaning, certainly, attains all auspiciousness and reaches Heaven, having his sins washed away by his knowledge.[1]

and

> What has been learned but not understood has to be spoken of as mere utterance; like dry fire-wood where there is no fire, it does not kindle in any way.[2]

condemn the man who simply knows the letter of the *Vedas* without having a knowledge of the meaning of the *Vedas*, and glorify persons who understand the meaning of the *Vedas*. This understanding of the meaning of the *Vedic* texts comes in as a natural step in the obligatory study of the *Vedas* under the teacher, in so far as the student has the needed equipment in language, in grammar, in Etymology (*Nirukta*), in

[1] स्थाणुरयं भारवाहः किलाभूदधीत्य वेदं न विजानाति योऽर्थम् ।
योऽर्थज्ञ इत सकलं भद्रमश्नुते नाकमेति ज्ञानविधूतपाप्मा ॥

[2] यदधीतमविज्ञातं निगदेनैव शब्द्यते ।
अनग्नाविव शुष्कैधो न तज्ज्वलति कर्हिचित् ॥

prosody etc. Thus Vācaspati Mis'ra says in his *Bhāmatī*:[1]

> Even prior to a desire to know ***Brahman***, to him who has studied the *Vedas* and who knows the relation of words with their meanings due to learning *Vedas*, Etymology, Grammar etc. there is the understanding of the nature of ***Brahman*** endowed with eternality etc. from texts beginning with "O gentle one, this was in the beginning even as existent" and ending with "That thou art," even without a critical investigation thoroughly.[2]

This investigation into the nature of ***Brahman*** is not obligatory for all. This is only for those who have the eligibility (*Adhikāra*). I have already stated the items of eligibility according to the *Advaita Vedānta*.

I am not sure if, in *Mīmāṁsā*, the critical investigation of the nature of *Dharma* is obligatory. The statement of S'abarasvāmin must be critically gone into. Does the "study" in the prescription of the study of what has been prescribed for one's own study contain the element of studying the meaning also? Or does it not? In both the cases there is only one course open and that is to return home from the teacher's household. After "study," one has to return home. There is

[1] *Bhāmatī* is a commentary on the *Bhāṣya* of S'aṅkarācārya on the *Vedānta Sūtras*.

[2] प्रागपि ब्रह्मजिज्ञासाया अधीतवेदस्य निगमनिरुक्तव्याकरणादिपरिशीलनविदितपद-तदर्थसंबन्धस्य सदेव सोम्येदमग्र आसीत् इत्युपक्रमात् तत्त्वमसि इत्यन्तात् सन्दर्भात् नित्यत्वाद्युपेतब्रह्मस्वरूपावगमस्तावदापाततो विचाराद्विनापि अस्ति ।

nothing more to be done at the teacher's household after that "study." So the statement of S'abarasvāmin: "but when the Veda has been studied, two courses are open" appears to have no basis.

S'abarasvāmin further says:

> Indeed it has a visible fruit, namely, the understanding of the rites. And the great people who are well-versed in *Yāgas* do not speak of the fruit merely from the study.[1]

From this passage we find that the understanding of the meaning is not the subject of a *Vedic* injunction. It is given here only as the convention among those who are well-versed in the *Yāgas*. Is not that understanding of the meaning contained in the study of what has been prescribed for one's own study itself, which comprehends the study of the auxiliary texts too? And nowhere has *Mīmāṁsā* been mentioned as a *Vedāṅga* (auxiliary text). Both in the *Nirukta* and in the *Mīmāṁsā Sūtras* all that is said is that the Deity etc. should be thought of as being reminded of by the *Mantra*, and for this purpose one must know the meaning of the *Mantra*. Pārthasārathi Mis'ra in his *S'āstradīpikā*[2] speaks of understanding of the meaning

[1] दृष्टो हि तस्यार्थः कर्मावबोधनं नाम। न च तत्राध्ययनमात्रात् तत्रभवन्तो याज्ञिकाः फलं समामनन्ति ।

[2] *S'āstradīpikā* is an interpretation of the *mīmāṁsā* system in which a group of *sūtras* forming a topic (*Adhikaraṇa*) is taken up for consideration. On this plan the entire text of the *sūtras* has been explained.

for which the study of the words of the texts is a part. He says:

> The study has been prescribed for the purpose of understanding the meaning of the text resulting in the order of learning the words. Therefore, since it is not possible without critical study, the critical study is prescribed even by the prescription of the study; hence, even staying at the teacher's household, the critical study of the meaning has to be conducted.[1] (I-1-1)

And he concludes:

> and in this way, the initiation is a part of the study in so far as it is a purification of the disciple who is the agent for the study which has a fruit; study too is for the purpose of the understanding of the meaning, which is a visible (fruit); but the understanding of the meaning, being of utility in the performance (of the *Yāgas*) has certainly the well-known fruit. In this way all have a fruit.[2] (I-1-1)

Pārthasārathi Mis'ra closely follows the words of the *Bhāṣya*. One has to consider if *Vicāra* (critical study) is necessary for the sort of understanding of the

[1] अक्षरग्रहणादिपरम्परोपजायमानवाक्यार्थज्ञानार्थं अध्ययनं विधीयते। ततस्तस्य विचारमन्तरेणासंभवात् अध्ययनविधिनैव अर्थाद्विचारो विहित इति गुरुगृहे एवावस्थाय विचारयितव्यो धर्मः।

[2] एवं च फलवदध्ययनकर्तृभूतमाणवकसंस्कारत्वात् उपनयनमध्ययनाङ्गम्। अध्ययनमपि दृष्टार्थज्ञानार्थम्। अर्थज्ञानं तु अनुष्ठानौपयिकत्वात् प्रसिद्धफलकमेव। इति सर्वेषां फलवत्त्वम्।

meaning that is mentioned here, or only the study of grammar etc.

The interpretation of Kumārila Bhaṭṭa in his *S'lokavārtika*[1] is very interesting. He finds great difficulty in accepting the words of the *Bhāṣya* text in many places, and yet his reverence to the great Teacher compels him to attempt at squeezing some consistent and sensible meaning out of the text of the *Bhāsya*. He definitely says that there is a conflict between critical study of the meaning, continuing the stay at the teacher's household, by the student on one side and his return home from the household of the teacher, if study means only the study of the words of the text. He says:

> If only the study of the text has been accomplished, then Ceremonial Bath is in conflict with this.[2] (I-91)

But he tries one explanation. The prescription, " One shall perform the Ceremonial Bath after study," does not mean mere study of the text, but also the understanding of its meaning:

> But there will be no (such) conflict if it be that "after study" means "after understanding."[3] (I-92)

Later he has a more interesting interpretation, which it is that is of use in the context here:

[1] *S'lokavārtika* is a critical exposition in verses (*s'lokas*) of the *Bhāṣya* of S'abarasvāmin on the *mīmāṁsā sūtras* for the 1st *Pāda* of the 1st *Adhyāya*.

[2] ग्रन्थग्रहणमात्रे च कृते स्नानं विरुध्यते ।

[3] अधीत्येत्यधिगम्येति व्याख्याने त्वविरोधिता ।

And here, it is the return from the household of the teacher as indicated by the Ceremonial Bath that can be in conflict as the contradictory ; but not the use of alcohol etc.[1] (I-100, 101)

Therefore, continuing in the household of the teacher, without avoiding alcohol, meat etc., there can be the desire to know (***Dharma***), not being in conflict ; so it is understood.[2] (I-101, 102)

And so long as the element of returning from the household of the teacher is not finished, the Ceremonial Bath is not finished, as that (Ceremonial Bath) expresses all this.[3] (I-102, 103)

If what is meant by the Ceremonial Bath is the return from the teacher's household, it is this return that is opposed to further study and critical investigation. Certain vows can be terminated after the study of the text. Then the various elements of what is meant by the Ceremonial Bath can be started, continuing the stay at the household of the teacher for the further critical study. Such relaxation in the disciplines is enjoined in the *Smṛtis* (Law Codes) :

Non-avoidance of alcohol, meat etc. which is enjoined in the *Smṛtis* and which has only an invisible

[1] स्नानोपलक्षिता चात्र निवृत्तिर्गुरुवेश्मन: ।
विरोधित्वेन बाध्येत ; न तु मध्वादिभक्षणम् ॥

[2] तस्माद्गुरुकुले तिष्ठन् मधुमांसाद्यवर्जयन् ।
जिज्ञासेताविरोधित्वाद्धर्ममित्यवगम्यते ॥

[3] गुरुगेहनिवृत्त्यंशो यावन्न च समाप्यते ।
तावत् सकलवाचित्वान्न स्नानं पर्यवस्यति ॥

> fruit: if the author of the *Sūtras* prohibit this too, he does not shine well.[1] (I-107)

Kumārila Bhaṭṭa raises the question whether the student cannot return from the teacher's household at the end of the study of the text and once more take up residence there for the critical study. He says that there is not sufficient evidence to make such an assumption. We have to presuppose some unseen fruit. And there is no need for such an assumption:

> What can be the taking up of residence by (the student) who desires to know (*Dharma*) after returning from the household of the teacher: for this too, there can be only an unseen fruit; therefore such is not the firm position here.[2] (I-108)

Thus Kumārila has to say that after the study of the text, he starts the elements constituting the Ceremonial Bath which ends with the final return from the household of the teacher, but which begins with the relaxation of certain disciplines.

I have cited this long passage from Kumārila Bhaṭṭa to show that he too makes a distinction between general study and critical study. There is a relaxation in the discipline after the general study, and during the further study of a critical nature. S'abarasvāmin

[1] स्मृतिप्राप्तमिदानीं तु मधुमांसाद्यवर्जनम् ।
प्रतिषेधन्नदृष्टार्थं सूत्रकारो न शोभते ॥

[2] निवृत्य गुरुवासाच्च जिज्ञासोर्यः पुनर्भवेत् ।
प्रवेशः, सोऽप्यदृष्टार्थः; इति नैवेह संस्थितिः ॥

and Pārthasārathi Mis'ra seem to accept a continous and uniform course of study until there is the understanding of the meaning too. To Kumārila Bhaṭṭa the study contemplated by the *Sūtra*, "Then therefore, the desire to know *Dharma*," is a distinct process, separated from the process contemplated by the prescription, "One shall study what has been prescribed for one's own study." Kumārila too takes this critical study as a part of the obligatory study.

In considering the distinction between the two parts of the study, namely the general study and the critical study, I must take up the rite called *Godāna*, which is prescribed in the *Gṛhya-Sūtras*. *Ās'valāyana-Gṛhya-Sūtra* describes the ceremony of *Caula* (first shaving and forming the tuft) in the 17th section of the first chapter, and in the next section, there is described the ceremony of *Godāna*. It begins :

> By this, *Godāna* (has been described).[1] (I-18-1)

Thus the ceremony is practically the same. The only difference is that where in *Caula* there is mention of hair on the head, here it must refer to the beard. Thus it is said :

> Where the word hair appears, one has to use the word beard.[2] (I-18-3)

Thus, this is the first shaving of the face and other parts of the body, while in *Caula*, it is only the head

[1] एतेन गोदानम् ।

[2] केशशब्दे तु श्मश्रुशब्दान् कारयेत् ।

that was shaved, as is natural in so far as at that age there would be hair only on the head. This ceremony is to be in the sixteenth year:

In the sixteenth year.[1] (I-18-2)

So says Ās'valāyana. On this point there is practical agreement among all the writers on the subject. There is a difference of opinion whether it is in the sixteenth year after conception or after birth. But this is a small matter. The commentators on Ās'valāyana say very little on the point at this stage. But when the question of the termination of study at the teacher's household came up for consideration, both the commentators cite a view that the time for this ceremony was in the sixteenth year after initiation (*Upanayana*). The passage was already cited in the first Lecture. The commentators also give it as another view that the ceremony is to be performed in the sixteenth year after birth.

In considering this question we must look into the details of the ceremony. The first step is prescribed in:

Here they moisten the beard.[2] (I-18-4)

The *Mantra* to be used for this is:

Purify his head and face; do not take away his life.[3] (I-18-5)

[1] षोडशे वर्षे ।

[2] श्मश्रूणीहोन्दति ।

[3] शुन्धि शिरो मुखम् । मास्यायुः प्रमोषी ।

Then there is the order to the barber :

> He arranges his hair, his beard, the hair (on the body) and his nails, ending in the north.[1] (I-18-6)

This is more or less the adaptation of the ceremonial for the first shaving of the hair and forming the tuft (*Cūlākarma*). I cite below the relevant parts from the description of the ceremony :

> To the west of (the boy) for whom (the ceremony) is to be performed (the father) stations himself and pours cold and warm water with (the words) " With water, O Vayu, come hither."[2] (I-17-6)
>
> Taking (parts) of that (water), (and) fresh butter or some drops of curds he moistens the (boy's) head three times from the left to the right with (the words) " May Aditi cut thy hair ; may the waters moisten thee for vigour."[3] (I-17-7)
>
> (With the words) " O razor, do not harm him ", with an iron razor.[4] (I-17-9)
>
> He cuts (the hair), (with the words) " The razor with which, in the beginning, Savitar, the knowing one, has shaved king Soma and Varuṇa, with that, O Brahmins, shave now his (hair) that he may be

[1] केशश्मश्रुलोमनखान्युदक्संस्थानि संप्रव्यति ।

[2] पश्चात्कारयिष्यमाणस्यावस्थाय शीतोष्णा अप: समानीयोष्णेन—वा य उदकेनेहि -इति ।

[3] तासां गृहीत्वा नवनीतं दधिद्रप्सान् वा प्रदक्षिणं शिरस्त्रिरुन्दति—अदिति: केशान् वपतु । आप उन्दन्तु वर्चसे—इति ।

[4] स्वधिते मैनं हिंसी:—इति लौहेन क्षुरेण ।

blessed with long life, till he becomes old."[1] (I-17-10)

Cutting and cutting, he gives (the hair) with their points to the east, together with *S'ami*[2] leaves, to the mother.[3] (1-17-11)

This is the ceremony of the first forming of the tuft on the head, and this same ceremony is to be followed in the *Godāna* also.

Is it possible to substitute the word "beard" for the word "hair" in this prescription and apply it to a youth of just sixteen? This point must be considered carefully. Does that youth have the beard at that age? If the ceremony is to be performed at the end of the course in the teacher's household at the age of twenty or twenty-four, *i.e.*, twelve or sixteen years after initiation, this is quite fitting. I must also note that this has dwindled into a very insignificant ceremony in later times and some of the latter-day authors do not even mention it.

There are other evidences also that make it impossible for this ceremony to have been performed at the age of sixteen. For example *Gobhila-Gṛhyasūtra* says in the first *Kaṇḍikā* of the third *Prapāṭhaka* that at this ceremony, all the hair on his body must be shaven and that during this ceremony, sexual intercourse must be avoided. Is this also a prescription for a

[1] प्रच्छिनत्ति—येनावपत् सविता क्षुरेण सोमस्य राज्ञो वरुणस्य विद्वान् । तेन ब्रह्माणो वपतेदमस्यायुष्माञ्जरदष्टिर्यथासत्—इति ।

[2] This is a kind of tree.

[3] प्रच्छिद्य प्रच्छिद्य प्रागग्राञ्छमीपर्णैः सह मात्रे प्रयच्छति ।

youth of sixteen or is it more appropriate for a youth towards the end of his educational course, say after his twentieth year?

When *Vedic* study was prescribed for twelve years, the commentators on the *Ās'valāyana-Gṛhya-Sūtra* said that *Godāna* comes sixteen years after initiation, twelve years being devoted for the study of the text and four years for *Mahānāmnī* etc. This was only one of the two views, the other being that *Mahānāmnī* etc. were included in the twelve years and that the *Godāna* was to be performed in the sixteenth year after birth, *i.e.*, eight years after initiation. There are certain ceremonies to be performed during the stay by the student at the teacher's household. There are four of them; there are slight differences among the authors on the subject. They are:

Ās'valāyana Smṛti: Mahānāmnī, Mahāvrata, Upaniṣad and Godāna.

Sāṅkhyāyana-Gṛhya-Sūtra: S'ukriya, S'ākvara, Vratika and Aupaniṣada. (II-11-12)

Gobhila: Godāna, Vratika, (Āditya), Aupaniṣada, Jyaiṣṭhyasāmika. (III-1-28)

In the commentary on the *As'valāyana-Gṛhya-Sūtra* when the twelve years of study was prescribed, there was a reference to the *Vratas* beginning with *Mahānāmnī*, that they are obligatory and shall not be given up, though in the case of those who have to give up a part, it is possible to give up a part of the earlier study of the texts.

This *Mahānāmnī* is described in detail in the *Gobhila-Gṛhya-Sūtra* in the second *Kaṇḍikā* of the third *Prapāṭhaka.* It is also mentioned in the 12th *Khaṇḍa* of the second *Adhyāya* in the *S'āṅkhyāyana-Gṛhya-Sūtra.* The *Mahānāmnī* is the name given to a few verses that appear in the *Aitareya-Āraṇyaka* IV and at the end of the *Pūrvārcika* of the Sāma-Veda[1] as a supplement. This *Vrata* also has dwindled into insignificance in latter days. These *Vratas* mark different stages in the higher studies of the *Vedas*, after the study of the text.

One thing is certain. When the disciple stays in the teacher's household, he first studies the text of the *Vedas* along with the *Vedāṅgas*, which training gives him an opportunity to understand the meaning of the texts of the Vedas also in a general way, and there are certain studies forming the closing portion of the course. There is a difference of opinion whether these closing courses form part of the twelve years of study or not. It is only the twelve years of study that is obligatory and as such there is also this possibility that such final courses were not obligatory according to certain views. According to *Mīmāmsā*, the critical study of the meaning of the *Vedas* (*Vicāra*) is obligatory and a student shall return from the household of the teacher only after such critical study, though according to Kumārila Bhaṭṭa, there can be relaxations of disciplines during

[1] The text of the Sāmaveda consists of the first (*Pūrva*) and the later collection of hymns (*Uttarārcika*).

this period of critical study. The shaving of the beard and hair on the body, in the ceremony of *Godāna*, is to be performed at a certain stage during the disciple's stay at the teacher's household. It looks as if it is sixteen years after his residence there, and not in his sixteenth year, *i.e.*, eight years after the commencement of his studies. The texts do not agree in details and the ceremony has become insignificant in actual practice. So it is not possible to get a clear picture of the situation. In this connection I may state that the ceremony is called *Godāna* in so far as the fee is a cow. The ceremony is also called *Keśānta* (end of wearing the hair on the head unshaven); this must be a part of the vow during the stay at the teacher's household.

There is no doubt about the fact that during the disciple's stay at the household of the teacher, there are two stages in his studies. One is a lower one and the other is a later and higher one. The latter course has relation to parts of the *Vedic* studies relating to the *Āraṇyaka* and the *Upaniṣad.* I am not far wrong if I equate these two stages with the modern secondary and college courses. What corresponds to the secondary stage was obligatory. What corresponds to the college course is also obligatory according to some of the schools of thought, although special eligibility for critical study contemplated in the *Vedānta Sūtra*, " Then therefore, the desire to know Brahman," has been prescribed according to certain Schools. The impression that I have been able to form is that even what corresponds to the college course of modern times was obligatory at a certain stage in the history of education in India; it may be a very early stage. Its traces are unmistakable in the literature available.

III. The Higher Stages in the Acquisition of Wisdom

In the list of subjects enumerated by Nārada when he approached Sanatkumāra, there are subjects included both in the secondary and in the college courses. The secondary course started with *Upanayana* (initiation), the parent taking the student to the teacher and admitting him into his household as a disciple. The college course is also included in this period of stay at the teacher's household, according to the majority of views reflected in the available literature.

There is a still higher study, and this study comes in after what is called *Upasadana* or the voluntary approach of a disciple to a teacher for higher knowledge on the subjects. It is this stage in the study that is found mentioned in various parts of the *Upaniṣad* texts. In the *Upaniṣads* we come across various stories of students seeking higher knowledge who approach a teacher for such higher instruction. The prohibition of imparting knowledge to those who do not seek it, may have special reference to this higher stage in teaching. It is true that in the *Upanayana* also, there is the element of seeking knowledge on the part of the student, through the parent who takes the student to the teacher's household. But in so far as that stage in education was obligatory, such a prohibition has no special significance.

The *Kenopaniṣad* starts with the following question :

> Urged by whom, directed by whom, does the mind fly? By whom joined does the primieval Breath proceed? By whom urged do they speak this word? And which God does join together the eye and the ear.[1] (I-1)

This is not definitely mentioned in the text itself as a question put by a student to any teacher. But actually it is so, and has been so explained by the commentators. The *Pras'nopaniṣad* is so called since it contains questions (*pras'nas*) put by disciples to a teacher :

> Sukes'as of the Bharadvāja Family, Satyakāma of the S'ibi family, Gārgya of the Family of Sūrya, Kausalya of the Family of Ās'valayāna, Kabandhi Kātyāyana of the Family of Bhṛgu—indeed these, keeping Brahman in view and firmly devoted to Brahman, seeking (knowledge of) the ultimate Brahman, they lo, with kindled fuel in their hands, approached the Lord Pippalāda, (being sure) that he certainly will tell (them) all about it.[2] (I-1)

[1] केनेषितं पतति प्रेषितं मनः केन प्राणः प्रथमः प्रैति युक्तः ।
केनेषितां वाचामिमां वदन्ति चक्षुः श्रोत्रं क उ देवो युनक्ति ॥

[2] सुकेशाश्च भारद्वाजः, शैब्यश्च सत्यकामः, सौर्यायणिश्च गार्ग्यः, कौसल्यश्चाश्वलायनः, भार्गवः कबन्धिः कात्यायनः—ते हैते ब्रह्मपरा ब्रह्मनिष्ठाः परं ब्रह्मान्वेषमाणाः, एष ह वै तत् सर्वं वक्ष्यति इति ते ह समित्पाणयो भगवन्तं पिप्पलादमुपसन्नाः ।

In the *Taittirīyopaniṣad*, Bhṛgu approaches his father Varuṇa for higher knowledge:

> Bhṛgu, son of Varuṇa, approached his father Varuṇa (with the request), " Teach me Brahman, O Lord."[1] (III-1)

There are various stories of disciples approaching a teacher for such higher knowledge in the *Chāndogya Upaniṣad*:

> Therefore Jānas'ruti of the family of Putra, having taken six hundred cows, a (necklace of) Niṣka (coin), and a carriage drawn by a pair of mules, went (to Raikva).[2] (Ch. Up. IV-2-1)
>
> Satyakāma, son of Jabālā. . . . went to Gautama, son of Haridrumata, and said.[3] (Ch. Up. IV-4-1-3)
>
> Upakosala, son of Kamalāyana, dwelt as a student in the house of Satyakāma, son of Jabālā; he tended his fires for twelve years; but though the teacher allowed the other students to depart, he did not allow him (Upakosala) to depart.[4] (Ch. Up. IV-101)
>
> There was S'vetaketu, son of Aruṇa. . . . He, lo, twelve years old, went (to his teacher) and at the

[1] भृगुर्वै वारुणिः वरुणं पितरमुपससाद अधीहि भगवो ब्रह्म इति ।

[2] तदु ह जानश्रुतिः पौत्रायणः षट् शतानि गवां निष्कमश्वतरीरथं तदादाय प्रतिचक्रमे ।

[3] सत्यकामो ह जाबालः . . . . हारिद्रुमतं गौतममेत्योवाच ।

[4] उपकोसलो ह वै कामलायनः सत्यकामे जाबाले ब्रह्मचर्यमुवास । तस्य ह द्वादश वर्षाण्यग्नीन् परिचचार । स ह स्मान्यानन्तेवासिनः समावर्तयन् । तं ह स्मैव न समावर्तयति ।

age of twenty four, studied all the *Vedas*, with a conceited mind and priding himself as a great exponent etc.[1] (Ch. Up. VI-1-1)

Nārada approached Sanatkumāra (with the request), "Teach me O Lord."[2] (Ch. VII-1-1)

These passages from the *Chāndogya Upaniṣad* indicate a higher stage in the education prevalent at that time in India, far above the education prescribed by the passage, "One shall study what has been prescribed for one's own study," "Then therefore, the desire to know *Dharma*" and "Then therefore, the desire to know *Brahman*." Since the texts available to us from those ages relate only to one subject, namely, the discussions about *Brahman*, we are able to know the facts only as relating to this field. Just as there are higher discussions about grammar indicated by the passage:

Then, there follows a treatment on Grammar[3] (*Mahābhāṣya*, beginning of Paspaśāhnika),

there must have been still higher specialised training in all the fields of knowledge current in those days. Thus the *Arthavicāra* (critical inquiry) found in the field of *Dharma* and *Brahman*, must have been current in all the subjects taught at that time, though we find actual texts only in a few specific subjects. The still higher specialised training too must have been current

[1] श्वेतकेतुर्हारुणेय आस। स ह द्वादशवर्ष उपेत्य चतुर्विंशतिवर्षः सर्वान् वेदानधीत्य महामना अनूचानमानी ... ।

[2] अधीहि भगव इति होपससाद सनत्कुमारं नारदः ।

[3] अथ शब्दानुशासनम् ।

for *Dharma*, Grammar etc. just as for *Brahman* recorded in the *Upaniṣads*. Of course, the *Brāhmaṇa* literature represents such higher discussion relating to *Yāgas*, corresponding to the *Upaniṣads* dealing with *Brahman*.

Above all these, there must have been discussions on the various subjects as we find in the *Bṛhadāraṇyaka Upaniṣad* :

> There was Dṛptabālāki, son of Garga, who was an exponent (of the wisdom). He said to Ajātaśatru, (king) of Kāśi.[1] (Bṛh. Up. II-1-1)

> Janaka, (king) of Videhas, performed a *Yāga* where many presents were given out. There were assembled in it Brahmins from the countries of the Kurus and Pāñcālas. To that Janaka, (king) of Videhas, there arose the desire to know this : " Who among these Brahmins may be the best exponent ? . . . He said to them, " O Lordly Brahmins, he who is the greatest among you may take away all these cows."[2] (Bṛh. Up. III-1-1)

Then there is the discussion in which Yājñavalkya took part,[3] which is very famous.

[1] दृप्तबालाकिर्हानूचानो गार्ग्य आस । स होवाचाजातशत्रुं काश्यम् ।

[2] जनको ह वैदेहो बहुदक्षिणेन यज्ञेनेजे । तत्र ह कुरुपाञ्चालानां ब्राह्मणा अभिसमेता बभूवुः । तस्य ह जनकस्य वैदेहस्य विजिज्ञासा बभूव । कः स्विदेषां ब्राह्मणानामनूचानतम इति । . . . . तान् होवाच—ब्राह्मणा भगवन्तो यो यो वसिष्ठः स एता गा उदाजतं इति ।

[3] Bṛh. Up. The whole of the third chapter.

IV. Closing Comments on the Main Issue

Now we must distinguish among the various stages in the education of the youth in ancient times, which has a close relation to the general educational set up in modern times. We can distinguish the following:

1. There is the primary stage before the initiation, when some training was given to the boy at home, consisting of writing, reading, language and literature, elements of grammar etc.

2. After this comes the initiation and the regular study in the household of the teacher after the ceremonial initiation, where the training in the proper recitation of the *Vedas* formed a very prominent part in the education, along with training in the auxiliary texts needed for the understanding of the *Vedic* texts (which include Phonetics, rules about *yāgas* and sacraments, Law, Grammar, Etymology, Prosody, Astronomy etc.) This education started at the age of eight and lasted for twelve years. This is obligatory.

3. The next stage was a continuation of the study at the household of the teacher, consisting of certain ceremonials like *Mahānāmnī*, and included certain higher aspects of study like the *Āraṇyakas* and *Upaniṣads*, *Mīmāṁsā* and *Vedānta*. This lasted for three or four years. There is a difference of view relating to the obligatory nature of this course. There is also a view that this course was included within the twelve years. This ended with the Ceremonial Bath marking the close of the study.

4. Still above this comes the very specialised study of certain specific problems. The student approaches a teacher for training in such subjects, and he receives such training, if he has the necessary qualifications, aptitudes and talents. For this there is no ceremonial initiation; the duration of the course too is not fixed.

5. The highest stage is marked by the meetings of Academies and Conferences where scholars assembled and discussed various problems.

V. Nature of the General Life of a Student

My main object in this course of two lectures is to consider the prescription of the study of what has been prescribed for one's own study, along with its various implications. But I cannot conclude the course without referring to a few other topics, which also arise out of this prescription of the study of what has been prescribed for one's own study. The life of the students must have been rather hard in such households of teachers. There were various restrictions on their daily life. Various amenities in life were denied to them. But we must understand that what can be called comfort and happiness in life is a purely subjective factor, and has only a relative value in one's life. Did they have palatial buildings for their education? Did they have luxurious furniture and other provisions? If such factors have to be taken into account in deciding the comforts of the students, it must be admitted that life in those days cannot at all be described as comfortable. But if we look at the problem from another angle, we will find that the students in those days were having a very cheerful life in the households of the teachers. They had their own recreations and occasions for relaxations. They had their needed diversions in life. They had holidays. If we examine the sort of life led by the students in the centres of education described in some literary specimens, it would be found, that, on the whole, the students were happy and contented. Look at the life which Kālidāsa describes in the hermitages of Kaṇva in the *S'ākuntala* and of Vasiṣṭha in the *Raghuvaṁs'a*. Look at the life in Vālmīki's hermitage as described in the *Uttararāmacarita* of Bhavabhūti. Look at the life described in the *Rāmāyaṇa* and in the *Mahābhārata*, in the various hermitages. We do not find any sign of moroseness; there was joy of a very high degree in all such places where students were living and receiving their education. After all, what we call modern comforts in life are really modern; in the European countries life in the monastries and in the educational centres were very hard indeed till very recent times.

In ancient India, all shared the life in the household of the teacher without any difference at all. Rich and poor had the same life. Princes and common people also lived together as brethren. They did not develop any sort of pessimism or aversion to life as a result of the hard life. They were awake to the realities of the ordinary world and to the needs of civic life. They developed into worthy citizens and the country prospered both in material wealth and spiritual eminence. The simple arrangements found in such educational institutions were in accord with the spirit of the times and were not fundamentals of education in those days.

VI. Forest Institutions for Education

It is held that the educational institutions in ancient India were situated in forests. It is not untrue of conditions at a later stage in the history of the country. I have already said that in the *Rigvedic* times, the *Ṛṣis* who composed the Hymns were the advanced citizens of the times. They did not live in the forests ; they lived in cities and in the country parts. As a matter of fact, forests play very little part in the life of the *Rigvedic* people. We see a lot of rivers and of ocean in the *Rigveda* ; but we see practically nothing of forests. In the description of the *Brahmacārin* in the *Atharvaveda*, there is no mention of the forest to which he was to retire, though that *Brahmacārin* represents one who devotes his life for the realisation of *Brahman*. But we see mention of ocean there :

> He immediately reaches the northern ocean from the eastern.[1] (XI-5-6)

and

> These, on the back of the flood, the *Brahmacārin* formed ; he practised penance, doing penance in the ocean.[2] (XI-5-26)

[1] स सद्य एति पूर्वस्मादुत्तरं समुद्रम् ।

[2] तानि कल्पाद्ब्रह्मचारी सलिलस्य पृष्ठे तपोऽतिष्ठत्तप्यमानः समुद्रे ।

But it is certain that in the *Taittirīyāraṇyaka*, the system of imparting education was shifted to the forests. In the *Upaniṣads* too, forests played a very important part in the educational set up of the times; the *Āśramas* of the *Ṛṣis* were in the forests. The *Gṛhya-Sūtras* mention a part of the study as what *has to be* imparted in the forest (*Āraṇyaka*) as distinct from what could be imparted in the villages (*Grāmya*). From the *Gṛhya-Sūtra*, it is found that it is only the final three or four years of study that has to be conducted in the forest, and not the entire study contemplated by the prescription of what has been prescribed for one's own study.[1] The *Āśrama* found described in the *Kāvyas* and *Nāṭakas* and in the *Purāṇas* were also in the forests.

But what are these forests? They are not the inaccessible jungles far away from human habitations. The *Taittirīyāraṇyaka* calls the place by the term *Acchadirdarśa* (a place from where the roofs of houses in the village cannot be seen). This cannot be very far from the habitations of men. The country must have been full of forests, unlike modern times when forests have been cleared. A more suitable term would be "penance groves" than "forest hermitages." The hermitages must have been established in groves of trees, on the banks of rivers and of lakes.

The *Maharṣis* were moving about from place to place in the afternoon. Thus when Duṣyanta reached the hermitage of Kaṇva in the afternoon during his

[1] See p. 24 above.

hunt, the *Maharṣi* had just left the hermitage on a pilgrimage:

> It is only just now that after entrusting his daughter S'akuntalā with the duty of entertaining guests, . . . he has gone to the Somatīrtha.[1] (Act I)

The *Maharṣis* went to the palaces of Kings for discussions. In all such cases they reach the hermitage back in the evening. This is also the picture that we find in the *Upaniṣads*. In the *Raghuvaṁs'a* too, we find that King Dilīpa started from his palace in the afternoon and reached the hermitage of Vasiṣṭha before sunset. In the *S'ākuntala*, it is found that the king could reach the palace from the hermitage of Kaṇva in an afternoon. Perhaps S'akuntalā and her companions too reached the palace of the king during a day's journey, starting in the forenoon and finishing the journey in the afternoon.

The hermitages were easily accessible by chariot. King Dilīpa went to the gate of Vasiṣṭha's hermitage in his chariot; Duṣyanta alighted from his chariot only at the gate of the hermitage of Kaṇva. In the *Uttararāmacarita*, Candraketu halted at the hermitage of Vālmīki. In the *Rāmāyaṇa*, Bharata went to see Rāma in the forest, after the death of Das'aratha, and he went in a chariot. In the *Mahābhārata*, when the Pāṇḍavas were in exile in the forest, where there were many hermitages, Duryodhana went there for his triumphant march (*Ghoṣayātrā*). Instances can be

[1] इदानीमेव दुहितरं शकुन्तलामतिथिसत्कारे नियुज्य . . . . सोमतीर्थं गतः ।

multiplied. But these are enough to show that the hermitages were not far away from cities and other habitations of men and were on the main roads, easily accessible even by chariots.

Thus it is found that educational institutions were situated on the highways from cities to cities, on the banks of rivers and of lakes, in peaceful groves of trees. Then there is the prescription of "begging" for the students as an obligatory part of their duties during their stay at the household of the teachers. Unless the hermitages were in the neighbourhood of human habitations, even habitations of rich men and of *Gṛhasthas* (householders), where were they to do their obligatory "begging"? And they had only the short afternoon or the morning for attending to such duties; they could not be absent from the hermitages for days together to collect the alms and bring them to the hermitage in a lump.

It is also doubtful if all the educational institutions were in the forests, even though forests were not far away from the cities and villages. Practically every scholar's home was a University. Such scholars lived as householders in their homes, in the cities and villages. Students also lived in such homes receiving education from such scholars.

It cannot also be asserted that the students left their own homes as little children of eight years, and later met their parents only as grown up men after twelve or even sixteen years, which is the period prescribed for the full course of study.

Can we say that in such an age of obligatory education, the homes contained only babies and grown up men without any boys and young men? Can we say that the parents were denied the pleasure of seeing their children when such children were developing their character and that the parents had no hand in shaping the tastes and aptitudes of their children? And what would the children be doing during the holidays, when studies were prohibited?

When we take all such points into consideration, the only conclusion possible is that the students were always nearby their parents. The household of the teachers were only the educational institutions. It may also be that the students boarded and lodged at such institutions even when the houses of their parents were not far away. They could always meet their parents, and they could enjoy the company of their parents at least during holidays. *Samāvartana* is not the *first* return of the students to the house of the parents after *Upanayana*; it is only the return of the students *after* the completion of their studies.

VII. Education of Women

There are many points that deserve consideration when one deals with the problem of education in ancient India, like professional, technical and vocational education. But I do not propose to enter into such details in this course, since nothing adequate can be done within the compass of the two lectures. But

I cannot ignore one aspect of education, namely, the education of women. In the *Rigveda* there is no indication of any disability attached to women regarding studies. Throughout the history of the country, women have been described as highly educated and cultured, in the entire literature. There is no heroine in any poem or drama who did not have a proper education. Anasūyā and Priyaṁvadā were receiving education in the hermitage of Kaṇva, and they refer to their equipment through such education :

> What state has been heard in the works on *Itihāsas* (epics) relating to those in love, such I find to be yours.[1] (Act III)
>
> By practice in drawing pictures, we will adorn the ornaments on your body.[2] (Act IV)

Sītā is not a docile heroine, submitting to her husband's decisions and to her own fate; in various situations, she argues her position with Rāma and with Lakṣmaṇa with great effect. When Yudhiṣṭhira pawned Draupadī at his game of gambling, she questioned the legal validity of the pawning, and none in the great assembly was able to answer her point. In the forest too, and also just prior to the great War, she was arguing matters of high state-craft with Yudhiṣṭhira and even with S'rī Krishna. Sāvitrī was able so to outwit Yama when her husband died that she was able even to recover him from the abode of

[1] यादृशीतिहासनिबन्धेषु कामयमानानामवस्था श्रूयते तादृशीं तव पश्यामि ।

[2] चित्रकर्मपरिचयेनाङ्गेषु ते आभरणविनियोगं कुर्वः ।

Yama. Instances can be given in hundreds about the high intellectual capacity and training of women and their cultural equipments.

But it has been found that at a later time, the ceremonial initiation and the prescribed study were denied to them. Perhaps education as such was not denied to women; yet there was a decline in the education of women in India in later times. It is the irony of the situation that although women were authors of some of the *Vedic* hymns, they were later denied the right to study the *Vedas*.

In the history of Pāṇinian interpretation also we see such a decline in the education of women. There is the *Sūtra* of Pāṇini :

> Also in the return address (by a teacher to the student etc.), except in the case of *S'ūdras*.[1]
>
> (VIII-2-83)

This is in considering the question of the prolongation of the vowel. The final syllable should be prolonged (*Pluta*) when there is the return address (*pratyabhivādana*) except when it is meant for a *S'ūdra*. Since *S'ūdras* do not know grammar and the proper use of accents and intonations, such niceties need not be observed. In Pāṇini, this exception is only for a *S'ūdra* ; but at a later time there is the emendation adding women also ; so says Patañjali in his *Mahābhāṣya* :

> For what purpose is it said "except in the case of a *S'ūdra*"? You fare well, O Tuṣajaka, (here,

[1] प्रत्यभिवादेऽशूद्रे ।

> the final syllable of the name Tuṣajaka, which is of a *S'ūdra*, need not be prolonged). Very little has been said by "except in the case of *S'ūdras.*" It should be said, "except in the case of *S'ūdras*, women and the malicious." [1]

Here women are put along with *S'ūdras* and with the malicious. *S'ūdras* do not have any familiarity with accent and intonation and the malicious do not deserve such courtesy. And women too are denied that decorum. This shows that there has been a sort of decadence in the social position of women and their educational equipment from the time of Pāṇini to the time of Kātyāyana, who wrote the first emendations to Pāṇini's grammar, and of Patañjali who gave the comprehensive exposition of Pāṇini, along with Kātyāyana's work.

Education under a certain prescription, which was meant for all citizens, both men and women belonging to all classes and communities, became restricted at a later stage to one community and also to the *men* in that community. There has been also a narrow-down in the range of education in course of time, from the *Vedic* age. But the *Upanayana* ceremony and the study as prescribed, and the *Upasadana* and the still higher aspect of discussions at Academies and Conferences continued unimpaired till very recent times. Now even that is experiencing a shaking.

[1] अशूद्रे इति किमर्थम् । कुशल्यसि तुषजक । अत्यल्पमिदमुच्यते अशूद्रे इति । अशूद्रस्त्र्यसूयकेषु इति वक्तव्यम् ।

VIII. Conclusion

In the course of the "evolution" of civilization in this world, our country which had this obligatory education prescribed for all citizens and practised by all citizens, came into contact with modern civilization, and within fifty years after such a contact and the introduction of a system of education calculated to lift up the nation from medieval ignorance and superstitions into modern enlightenments, leaders of the country had to start an agitation for the spread of ***elementary*** education ; even now universal basic education is only an ideal kept in view, perhaps to be accomplished within a few years.

At present it is doubtful if there is another calling in India more neglected and more despised than that of a teacher. But, in ancient times, the teacher was the most honoured citizen of the country. The destiny of the country was placed in the hands of those who had sat at the feet of such revered scholars and who consequently developed a veneration for the teaching profession and for scholarship and wisdom represented by this profession. Practically the wise man, the learned man, the scholar, the teacher, ruled the country. Every one bowed his head before the man of wisdom. This pre-eminent position assigned to the teachers created an unshakable unity in the country based on culture and a realisation of certain higher fundamental values in things. Problems were discussed and settled by wise men on academic standards. There is no other country that has developed the conception of the "*Śiṣṭas*," *i.e.* those who could not make a mistake in the matter of the relation of actions and their fruits, who could not be suspected of any personal motive in their public activities, who were actuated only by the one motive of protection, preservation and propagation of *Dharma* among men. Both legislation and administration of justice were above the general civil adiministration of the country; it was in the hands of the wise men, who were above political states and parties in states.

My main object in preparing this lecture is to show that even in the modern civilized days, the prescription, "One shall study what has been prescribed for one's own study" and the final instruction given by the teacher to the disciples at the termination of their course of studies, "Speak the truth, observe *Dharma* in your conduct" have a great value and can serve our purpose, properly adjusted to the needs of the changed times. The changes are only in details, and the fundamentals can remain and can also serve as models for the rebuilding of a new system of educational set-up in other countries.

तेजस्वि नावधीतमस्तु । मा विद्विषावहै ॥

PUBLICATIONS OF THE ADYAR LIBRARY

(The Theosophical Society, Adyar, Madras, 20, India)

		Rs.	A.
1910—1	A PRELIMINARY LIST OF THE SAMSKṚT AND PRĀKṚT MSS in the Adyar Library (Saṁskṛt-Devanāgarī) Boards Rs 1-8 Cloth	2	0
1912—2.	A DESCRIPTIVE CATALOGUE OF THE SAMSKṚT MSS in the Adyar Library *By* F O. Schrader, Vol I, Upaniṣads Cloth ..	5	0
3.	THE MINOR UPANIṢADS (Saṁskṛt) critically edited for the Adyar Library. *By* F. O. Schrader, Vol. I —Saṁnyāsa Cloth ...	10	0
1916—4.	AHIRBUDHNYA-SAṀHITĀ OF THE PĀÑCARĀTRA ĀGAMA (Saṁskṛt) 2 Vols Cloth ...	10	0
5	INTRODUCTION (English) TO THE PĀÑCARĀTRA AND THE AHIRBUDHNYA SAṀHITĀ. *By* F O. Schrader. Cloth ..	3	0
1920—6.	YOGA UPANIṢADS 20—with the Commentary of S'rī Upaniṣad-Brahma-Yogin Edited *by* Paṇḍit A. Mahadeva Sastri ..	5	0
1921—7	SĀMĀNYA VEDĀNTA UPANIṢADS 24—with the Commentary of S'rī Upaniṣad Brahma Yogin. Edited *by* Paṇḍit A. Mahadeva Sastri ..	5	0
1923—8.	VAIṢṆAVA UPANIṢADS 14—with the Commentary of S'rī Upaniṣad-Brahma-Yogin. Edited *by* Paṇḍit A, Mahadeva Sastri ..	4	0
1925—9.	S'AIVA UPANIṢADS 15—with the Commentary of S'rī Upaniṣad Brahma Yogin. Edited *by* Paṇḍit A. Mahadeva Sastri (Reprinted 1950) ..	5	8
10	S'ĀKTA UPANIṢADS 8—with the Commentary of S'rī Upaniṣad Brahma Yogin. Edited *by* Paṇḍit A Mahadeva Sastri (Reprinted 1950) ...	3	8
1926—11.	CATALOGUE OF SAMSKṚT MSS. in the Adyar Library (Revised). 2 Vols. Each ..	3	12
1929—12.	SAṀNYĀSA UPANIṢADS 17—with the Commentary of S'rī Upaniṣad-Brahma-Yogin. Edited *by* T R. Chintamani, and the Paṇḍits of the Adyar Library ...	4	0
13.	RUKMIṆĪKALYĀṆA-MAHĀKĀVYA by Rājacūḍāmaṇi-Dīkṣita Edited *by* the Paṇḍits of the Adyar Library and T. R. Chintamani ...	2	0

		Rs.	A.
1933—14.	UNPUBLISHED MINOR UPANIṢADS with the Commentary of S'rī Upaniṣad-Brahma-Yogin. Edited *by* the Paṇḍits of the Adyar Library ...	5	0
1936—15.	TEN MAJOR UPANIṢADS with the Commentary of S'rī Upaniṣad-Brahma-Yogin. Edited *by* the Paṇḍits of the Adyar Library		
	Īs'a to Aitareya, Vol. I ...	4	8
	Chāndogya and Bṛhadāraṇyaka, Vol. II ...	6	0
	Vols 1 and 2, Boards ...	9	8
1937—16.	MELARĀGAMĀLIKĀ of Mahāvaidyanātha S'ivan Edited *by* Paṇḍit S. Subrahmanya Sastri ...	2	0
1938—17.	SAṀGRAHACŪḌĀMAṆI—Edited *by* Paṇḍit S Subrahmanya Sastri ...	5	0
18.	PRATYABHIJÑĀHṚDAYA (The Secret of Recognition) with English Translation and Notes *by* K F. Leidecker ...	3	0
19.	BHAVASAṄKRĀNTI-SŪTRA AND NĀGĀRJUNA'S BHAVASAṀKRĀNTI S'ĀSTRA—with the Commentary of Maitreyinātha —with English Translation *by* Paṇḍit N Aiyaswami Sastri ...	2	4
20	YOGA UPANIṢADS Translated into English *by* T. R. Srinivasa Aiyangar and Paṇḍit S. Subrahmanya Sastri ..	5	0
21	* WHERE THEOSOPHY AND SCIENCE MEET (in four Parts) by a body of experts—Edited *by* Professor D D. Kanga		
	Parts 1 and 2 Nature and Man ...	9	0
	Part 3. God—From Humanity to Divinity ...	2	8
	Part 4. Some Practical Applications	2	8
1939—22.	ṚGVEDAVYĀKHYĀ, MĀDHAVAKṚTĀ—Edited *by* Prof. C. Kunhan Raja. Vol. I ...	6	0
1940—23.	THE NUMBER OF RASAS *by* V. Raghavan, Department of Saṁskṛt, University of Madras ...	3	0
1941—24.	SĀMĀNYA VEDĀNTA UPANIṢADS—Translated into English *by* T. R Srinivasa Aiyangar and Paṇḍit S Subrahmanya Sastri ...	5	0
25.	BHAGAVADGĪTĀRTHAPRAKĀS'IKĀ of S'rī Upaniṣad-Brahmayogin (Saṁskṛt). Edited *by* the Paṇḍits of the Adyar Library ...	4	0
26.	SĀMAVEDA-SAṀHITĀ—With the Commentaries of Mādhava and Bharatasvāmin. Edited *by* Prof. C. Kunhan Raja ...	6	0
27.	RĀJA DHARMA (Dewan Bahadur K. Krishnaswami Rao Lectures, 1938, University of Madras) *by* Rao Bahadur K. V. Rangaswami Aiyangar ...	3	8

Published under the auspices of the Adyar Library Association.

Year	No.	Title	Rs.	A.
	28.	VARIVASYĀRAHASYA of Bhāsurānandanātha (Second Edition—Reprinted, 1948) Edited *by* Paṇḍit S Subrahmanya Sastri (with English Translation Etc) .	5	0
	29.	VYAVAHĀRANIRṆAYA OF VARADARĀJA—Edited *by* Rao Bahadur K. V. Rangaswami Aiyangar and A. N. Krishna Aiyangar ...	15	0
	30.	SAṀGĪTARATNĀKARA—With the Commentaries of Catura Kallināth and Siṁhabhūpāla Edited *by* Paṇḍit S Subrahmanya Sastri. Vol I (Adhyaya 1) ...	9	0
1942—	31.	CATALOGUE OF THE ADYAR LIBRARY, Western Section, Part 1 ...	5	0
	32.	ĀLAMBANAPARĪKṢĀ AND VṚTTI *by* Dinnāga Edited with English translation, Tibetan text etc *by* Paṇḍit N Aiyaswami Sastri ...	3	8
	33	SOME CONCEPTS OF ALAṀKĀRA-S'ĀSTRA *by* V Raghavan, University of Madras ...	4	0
	34.	VEDĀNTAPARIBHĀṢĀ—with English translation and Notes *by* Prof S S Suryanarayana Sastri	2	12
	35.	DESCRIPTIVE CATALOGUE of the Sanskrit Manuscripts in the Adyar Library *by* K Madhava Krishna Sarma Vol. I—Vedic .	15	0
	36.	S'RĪ PĀÑCARĀTRA-RAKṢĀ of S'ri Vedanta-Des'ika—Edited *by* Vaidyaratna Paṇḍit M. Duraiswami Aiyangar and Vedānta S'iromaṇi T Venugopalacharya	1	8
	37.	CATALOGUE OF THE ADYAR LIBRARY, Western Section, part 2 ...	6	0
	38.	CATURDAS'ALAKṢAṆĪ OF GADĀDHARA with three commentaries—Edited *by* Paṇḍit N Santanam Aiyar. Vol I ...	4	8
1943—	39.	PHILOSOPHY OF VIS'IṢṬĀDVAITA *by* Prof. P. N. Srinivasachari ...	10	0
	40.	VĀDĀVALĪ OF JAYATĪRTHA. Edited with English translation and Notes *by* P. Nagaraja Rao ..	4	0
	41.	SPINOZIAN WISDOM OR NATURAL RELIGION *by* James Arther ...	2	12
	42.	UṢĀNIRUDDHA of Rāmapāṇivāda. Edited *by* Paṇḍit S. Subrahmanya Sastri and Prof C. Kunhan Raja ...	3	8
1944—	43.	SAṀGĪTARATNĀKARA—With the Commentaries of Catura Kallinātha and Siṁhabhūpāla Edited *by* Paṇḍit S Subrahmanya Sastri. Vol II (Adhyāyas 2—4) ...	9	0
	44.	ĀS'VALĀYANAGṚHYASŪTRA—With the Commentaries of Devasvāmin and Nārāyaṇa. Edited *by* Svami Ravi Tirtha. Vol. I (Adhyāya 1) ..	6	4

		Rs.	A.
45.	ALPHABETICAL INDEX OF SANSKRIT MANUSCRIPTS in the Adyar Library ...	10	0
46.	CATALOGUE OF THE ADYAR LIBRARY, Western Section, Part 3 ...	7	0
47.	ĀTMAN IN PRE-UPANIṢADIC VEDIC LITERATURE *by* H. G. Narahari ...	8	0
1945—48.	RĀGAVIBODHA OF SOMANĀTHA with his own commentary Viveka. Edited by Paṇḍit S Subrahmanya Sastri ...	6	0
49	ACYUTARĀYĀBHYUDAYA OF RĀJANĀTHA ḌIṆḌIMA—Sargas 7 to 12. Edited *by* A. N Krishna Aiyangar ...	3	8
50.	ANCIENT WISDOM OF WALES *by* D. Jeffrey Williams ...	1	4
51.	SAṀGĪTARATNĀKARA OF S'ĀRṄGADEVA—Vol. I. Chapter I. English Translation *by* Prof. C Kunhan Raja. Cloth Rs 4-8 Boards ...	4	0
52	VAIṢṆAVA UPANIṢADS Translated into English *by* T. R. Srinivasa Aiyangar and G. Srinivasa Murti ...	10	0
1946—53.	NYĀYAKUSUMĀÑJALI of Udayanācārya—Translated into English *by* Svami Ravi Tirtha. (Vol. I– Books i and ii)...	4	0
54.	PRĀKṚTAPRAKĀS'A OF VARARUCI with the Commentary of Rāmapāṇivāda. Edited *by* Prof. C. Kunhan Raja and Paṇḍit K. Ramachandra Sarma ...	4	4
55.	SPHOṬAVĀDA OF NĀGES'A—Edited *by* Paṇḍit V. Krishnamacharya with his own Commentary ...	3	12
1947—56.	THE CRADLE OF INDIAN HISTORY *by* C R Krishnamacharlu ...	3	8
57.	UNMATTARĀGHAVA OF VIRŪPĀKṢA—Edited *by* Paṇḍit V. Krishnamacharya ...	1	12
58.	ORIGIN AND SPREAD OF THE TAMILS (Sankara-Parvati Lectures, 1940, University of Madras) *by* V. R Ramachandra Dikshitar ...	3	8
59.	JĪVĀNANDANAM OF ĀNANDARĀYAMAKHIN. Edited *by* Vaidyaratna Paṇḍit M. Duraiswami Aiyangar with his own Commentary ...	20	0
60.	DESCRIPTIVE CATALOGUE of Sanskrit MSS. in the Adyar Library, *by* Paṇḍit V. Krishnamacharya, Vol. VI—Grammar, Prosody and Lexicography ...	25	0
61.	ṚGVEDAVYĀKHYĀ of Mādhava, Vol. II, edited by Prof. C. Kunhan Raja ...	15	0
62.	DESCRIPTIVE CATALOGUE OF PALI MSS. in the Adyar Library, *by* Dr. E. W. Adikaram ...	6	0
1948—63.	HARICARITA OF PARAMES'VARA—Edited *by* Paṇḍit V Krishnamacharya with his own Commentary ...	5	0

		Rs	A.
64	GAUTAMA-DHARMASŪTRA-PARIŚIṢṬA (Second Praśna)—Edited *by* A. N. Krishna Aiyangar ...	9	0
65	SAMKALPASŪRYODAYA OF ŚRĪ VEṄKAṬANĀTHA with the Commentaries Prabhāvilāsa and Prabhāvali. Edited *by* Paṇḍit V. Krishnamacharya Part I ..	15	0
	Part II ..	15	0
	Reprint of No. 28—VARIVASYĀRAHASYA of Bhāsurānandanātha—Edited by Paṇḍit S. Subrahmanya Sastri (with English translation, Etc.) ...	5	0
1949—66	INDIAN CAMERALISM (A Survey of some aspects of Arthaśāstra) *by* K. V. Rangaswami Aiyangar	7	0
	Second Edition—Revised and Enlarged—of No. 21—WHERE THEOSOPHY AND SCIENCE MEET (Parts 1 and 2, Nature and Man) by a body of Experts, Edited *by* Prof. D. D. Kanga ..	9	0
67	TIRUKKUṞAL OF TIRUVALḶUVAR—(In Roman Transliteration) with English Translation by Prof. V. R. Ramachandra Dikshitar ..	3	0
68.	TIRUKKUṞAL OF TIRUVALLUVAR, with English Translation *by* Prof. V. R. Ramachandra Dikshitar	3	0
69.	CATALOGUE OF THE ADYAR LIBRARY, Western Section, part 4 (French)	1	12
70.	ALAMKĀRASAMGRAHA by Amṛtānandayogin. Edited *by* Paṇḍit V. Krishnamacharya and Paṇḍit K. Ramachandra Sarma ...	9	0
71	YĀJÑIKYUPANIṢAD VIVARAṆAM BY PURUṢOTHAMĀNANDA TĪRTHA—Edited *by* Paṇḍit V. Krishnamacharya and Paṇḍit K. Ramachandra Sarma ...	2	8
1950—72.	EDICTS OF AŚOKA (Priyadarśin) With English Translation *by* G. Srinivasa Murti and A. N. Krishna Aiyangar Boards Rs. 2-0. Cloth ..	3	0
73.	SOME ASPECTS OF EDUCATION IN ANCIENT INDIA (Dewan Bahadur K. Krishnaswami Rao Endowment Lectures, University of Madras, 1949) *by* Prof. C. Kunhan Raja ...	2	8
	Reprint of No. 9 ŚAIVA UPANIṢADS 15—with the commentary of Śrī Upaniṣad Brahma Yogin—Edited *by* Paṇḍit A. Mahadeva Sastri	5	8
	Reprint of No. 10. ŚĀKTA UPANIṢADS. 8—with the commentary of Śrī Upaniṣad Brahma Yogin—Edited *by* Paṇḍit A. Mahadeva Sastri	3	8

PAMPHLETS

Rs. A.

1939

VARIANT VERSION OF THE EKĀGNIKĀṆḌA. (Reprinted from the Adyar Library Bulletin, October, 1939). Edited *by* K. Madhava Krishna Sarma ... 0 3

1940

RĀJAMṚGĀṄKA OF BHOJA. (Reprinted from the Adyar Library Bulletin, October, 1940). Edited *by* K Madhava Krishna Sarma 0 4

1942

ṢAṬPAÑCĀS'IKĀ, a S'ilpas'āstra manual. (Reprinted from the Adyar Library Bulletin. February, 1942). Edited *by* K. Madhava Krishna Sarma . 0 5

PRAMĀṆAMAÑJARĪ OF SARVADEVA. (Reprinted from the Adyar Library Bulletin, May, 1942). Edited *by* K. Madhava Krishna Sarma . 0 6

A LIST OF MANUSCRIPTS. (Reprinted from the Adyar Library Bulletin, October, 1942) ... 1 0

THE PATH OF GREATNESS. (Reprinted from the Adyar Library Bulletin, December, 1942), *by* Dr. G. S. Arundale ... 0 6

1943

VIS'EṢĀMṚTA of Tryambaka Mis'ra. (An orthographical lexicon), Edited *by* H. G. Narahari. (Reprinted from the Adyar Library Bulletin, May, 1943) ... 0 12

A SANSKRIT LETTER OF MOHAMAD DARA SHUKOH with English Translation and Notes *by* Prof. C. Kunhan Raja (Reprinted from the Adyar Library Bulletin, October, 1940, May and October, 1943) ... 0 12

1946

DHARMACAURYARASĀYANA OF GOPĀLAYOGĪNDRA—Edited *by* H. G. Narahari (Reprinted from the Adyar Library Bulletin, October and December, 1946) ... 1 12

1948

SAṀSKṚTAGRANTHIVIGHAṬANA—*by* Prof. C. Kunhan Raja ... 0 8

CANDRAVĀKYAS OF VARARUCI—Edited *by* Prof C. Kunhan Raja with Appendices ... 2 0

BHĀRATA-RĀṢṬRA-SAṄGHAṬANĀ (Indian Constitution in Sanskrit verses)—a sample—*by* Prof. C. Kunhan Raja . 1 0

LANGUAGE PROBLEM IN INDIA—(Reprint from the Adyar Library Bulletin, Vol. XII, Part 4, December, 1948) .. 1 0

SANSKRIT IN INDIA—*by* G. Srinivasa Murti. (Reprint from the Adyar Library Bulletin, Vol. XII, Part 3, October, 1948) ... 1 0

INFLUENCE OF INDIAN THOUGHT ON FRENCH LITERATURE—*by* Prof. Louis Renou. (Reprint from the Adyar Library Bulletin, Vols. XII and XIII) ... 0 12

Rs A.

1949

THE FUTURE ROLE OF SANSKRIT (Sanskrit Language)—*by* C. Kunhan Raja. (Reprint from the Adyar Library Bulletin, Vol. XIII, Part 1, February, 1949) ... 0 12

THE FUTURE ROLE OF SANSKRIT (Sanskrit Literature, Sanskrit Scholarship and Sanskrit Scholars) *by* Louis Renou and C. Kunhan Raja ... 1 8

DAS'AKUMĀRAKATHĀSĀRA OF APPAYĪMĀTYA—Edited *by* H G Narahari ... 1 0

BRAHMASŪTRABHĀṢYA-SIDDHĀNTASAMGRAHA *by* S'ri Upaniṣad-brahmayogin—Edited by Pandit V. Krishnamacharya (Reprint from the Adyar Library Bulletin, Vol. XIII Parts 2 and 3) . 1 8

INDIA'S CULTURAL ROLE IN THE WORLD *by* C Kunhan Raja (Reprint from the Adyar Library Bulletin, Vol XIII, Part 4) . 0 12

1950

PĀDAVIDHĀNA OF S'AUNAKA with Bhāṣya—Edited *by* H G Narahari. (Reprint from the Adyar Library Bulletin, Vols XIII and XIV) 1 0

HINDU RELIGION AND HINDU CUSTOMS—*by* C. Kunhan Raja 0 8

IN THE PRESS

S'AIVA AND S'ĀKTA UPANIṢAḌS—Translated into English *by* T R. Srinivasa Aiyangar and Edited *by* G Srinivasa Murti.

YOGA UPANIṢADS—Translated into English *by* T. R Srinivasa Aiyangar and Edited *by* G Srinivasa Murti (Second Edition).

CATURDAS'ALAKSAṆĪ OF GADĀDHARA with three commentaries Vol. II *by* Paṇḍit N. Santanam Aiyar

ĀPASTAMBASMṚTI—Edited *by* A. N Krishna Aiyangar

SAMGĪTARATNĀKARA—With the Commentaries of Catura Kallinātha and Simhabhūpāla. Edited *by* Paṇḍit S. Subrahmanya Sastri, Vol III

HORĀS'ĀSTRA—with the commentary Apūrvārthapradars'ikā *by* A. N Srinivasaraghava Aiyangar

SĀLISTAMBASŪTRA—Restored from Tibetan and Chinese Sources—*by* Paṇḍit N. Aiyaswami Sastri.

SAMGĪTARATNĀKARA, English Translation—Vol. II, *by* Prof. C Kunhan Raja.

DESCRIPTIVE CATALOGUE of Sanskrit MSS in the Adyar Library, *by* H. G. Narahari, Vol V—Poetry, Drama and Poetics

ARISTOTLE'S KATHARSIS AND BHARATA'S STHĀYIBHĀVAS *by* Prof. C. Kunhan Raja

LANGUAGE—BARRIER OR BRIDGE *by* A Sita Devi

ṚGVEDABHĀṢYA OF SKANDASVĀMIN—Edited by Prof C. Kunhan Raja.

VEDĀNTAKĀRIKĀVALĪ OF VENKAṬĀCĀRYA—Edited *by* Pandit V. Krishnamacharya with his own Commentary and Translation

READY FOR THE PRESS

ĀŚVALĀYANAGṚHYASŪTRA with the Commentaries of Devasvāmin and Nārāyaṇa. Vol. II. Edited *by* Svami Ravi Tirtha.

NYĀYAKUSUMĀÑJALI OF UDAYANA with the Commentary of Varadarāja. Edited *by* Prof. C. Kunhan Raja.

CATURDAŚALAKṢAṆĪ OF GADĀDHARA—with Commentaries—Edited *by* Paṇḍit N. Santanam Aiyar, Vol. III.

PAKṢATĀ OF GADĀDHARA—with four commentaries Edited *by* Paṇḍit N. Santanam Aiyar.

SIDDHĀNTALAKṢAṆAM OF GADĀDHARA with commentaries. Edited *by* Paṇḍit N. Santanam Aiyar.

AVAYAVA OF GADĀDHARA—with commentaries. Edited *by* Paṇḍit N. Santanam Aiyar.

SĀMĀNYANIRUKTI OF GADĀDHARA with commentaries. Edited *by* Paṇḍit N. Santanam Aiyar.

VYUTPATTIVĀDA OF GADĀDHARA with commentaries. Edited *by* Paṇḍit N. Santanam Aiyar

TEN MAJOR UPANIṢADS—English Translation *by* T R. Srinivasa Aiyangar—Edited *by* G. Srinivasa Murti.

DESCRIPTIVE CATALOGUE OF SANSKRIT MSS. in the Adyar Library, *by* Pandit V Krishnamacharya. Vol, IX—Mīmāṁsā and Advaita-Vedānta